TEACHING HOW TO LEARN IN A WHAT-TO-LEARN CULTURE

KATHLEEN RICARDS HOPKINS

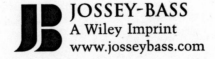

JOSSEY-BASS
A Wiley Imprint
www.josseybass.com

Published by Jossey-Bass
A Wiley Imprint
989 Market Street, San Francisco, CA 94103-1741—www.josseybass.com

Jossey-Bass books and products are available through most bookstores. To contact Jossey-Bass directly call our Customer Care Department within the U.S. at 800-956-7739, outside the U.S. at 317-572-3986, or fax 317-572-4002.

Illustrations (except for Figures 4.2, 7.2, and 9.2) hand drawn and inked by Jim Swanson at Heckle and Jive Productions, San Francisco, CA.

Jossey-Bass also publishes its books in a variety of electronic formats. Some content that appears in print may not be available in electronic books.

Library of Congress Cataloging-in-Publication Data
Hopkins, Kathleen Ricards, 1944-
    Teaching how to learn in a what-to-learn culture / Kathleen Ricards Hopkins.
        p. cm.
    Includes bibliographical references and index.
    ISBN 978-0-470-34352-4 (pbk.)
    1. Cognitive learning. 2. Learning—Study and teaching. 3. Learning, Psychology of. 4. Teaching. I. Title.
    LB1590.3.H675 2010
    370.15'2—dc22
                                                                    2009046004

10 9 8 7 6 5 4 3

CONTENTS

ABOUT THE AUTHOR

Dr. Kathleen Ricards Hopkins has been actively involved in the field of education for over thirty years. She received her undergraduate degree in education from the University of Delaware, her master's degree in education from Regent University in Virginia Beach, Virginia, and her doctorate in education from the College of William and Mary in Williamsburg, Virginia. Since 1991, Dr. Hopkins has been the executive director of the National Institute for Learning Development (NILD) based in Norfolk. She presents workshops nationally and internationally on topics related to the enhancement of learning ability. She was instrumental in establishing NILD community-based centers serving students of all ages who desire to go beyond tutoring and develop their abilities to learn.

To my family of educators:
Ralph, Susannah, Kristin

ABOUT THE NATIONAL INSTITUTE FOR LEARNING DEVELOPMENT

The National Institute for Learning Development (NILD) is a not-for-profit organization whose mission is to build competence and confidence in those who desire to improve their ability to learn. Nationally accredited by the Accrediting Council for Continuing Education and Training (ACCET), NILD trains teachers to improve their craft in teaching *how* to learn, not just what. Numerous dissertations have been written affirming the effectiveness of NILD's methods. Since 1982, NILD has trained thousands of teachers who have used its methods with tens of thousands of students. Transformed lives speak most clearly of the success of NILD's mission.

FOREWORD

In July of 1993, the author of this book came to Israel to participate in our annual international *Shoresh* training seminars. She was the Director of NILD and a member of the Professional Support Team from the NILD (the National Institute of Learning Development—formerly the National Institute of Learning Disabilities). The group numbered approximately twenty individuals, comprising the leadership of that organization. I knew of them well before this event, but was pleased to receive them, and understood what their participation meant. During the years preceding, and in the time since, I was quite aware of how the NILD activities paralleled in many ways the development and implementation of our theory and approaches. They represented the "content" side of the dilemma of learning disability, while we were emphasizing the "process" side. For these reasons, and others, I am pleased to be asked to write a foreword to this important book.

While it is personally gratifying to be quoted directly as much as I am in this volume, and to have so much of what the author develops in the text attributed to my theory, it is more important to reflect that this book is a manifestation and materialization of where the NILD has been going, and how its development reflects so much of what is important to me.

It was my feeling as I interacted with the NILD team in 1993, and has been confirmed in the years since, that they were searching for a coherent theory to provide a foundation for their intuitively arrived at therapeutic techniques. Early in the development of the teaching techniques of the NILD, as they were influenced and taught by Deborah Zimmerman, it was understood that they were, to paraphrase and quote Grace Mutzabaugh (1999) in her history of the NILD, doing something much more than "academic skills" tutoring. According to her, the techniques of educational therapy that are applied by NILD therapists have as their primary value the stimulation of deficit areas in the brain. The goal is not to enhance content, but to "change areas of the brain that had not yet developed or were lying dormant" . . . "as the deficient auditory and visual/perceptual were stimulated, the cognitive areas of the brain, where higher level thinking takes place, would also be stimulated" (p. 43).

From this point of view, the title and content of this book become critically important. It requires that we think about the process of learning and the structure of educational enterprises from a *cognitive* perspective. In this context, the theory of structural cognitive modifiability (SCM) and its constructs of the *deficient cognitive functions*, the *cognitive map*, and the *parameters of mediated learning experience* (MLE) provide a very specific and functionally operational basis for grounding what is learned, why it is learned, and how the learning can be applied to new learning and the demands of a changing environment. Moreover, as our theory and applied systems—the Learning Propensity Assessment Device (LPAD) and the Feuerstein Instrumental Enrichment (FIE) program—have developed and been used throughout the world with a wide diversity of populations, the basic premise that underlies them, the modifiability of human functioning through the changing of brain structures, has received strong confirmation by the new neurophysiological research. We now know that the brain is the most plastic of human organs, and that plasticity can and must be achieved through cognitively oriented interventions. The title and theme of this book directly relate to the implications of this state of affairs—that we must find ways of teaching learners how to think.

In a paper titled *Thinking to Learn; Learning to Think* (Feuerstein and Falik, forthcoming), the limitations of the teaching of content knowledge are described, and the need to teach learners how to acquire rules and strategies of thinking that can then be applied to specific content is emphasized. We emphasize that the demands of the modern world require that learners be adaptive and creative, and that the human organism is modified by exposure to cognitively oriented stimulation, presented in the context of a mediational learning experience, rather than the simple transmission of knowledge, skills, or learning habits. The dynamic for this learning process is exposure to a very systematic and focused interaction that we have called mediated learning experience (MLE). The learner is engaged in a systematic interaction with a concerned and focused teacher or parent who interposes him/herself in the learning situation, makes that which is experienced meaningful. Of particular relevance to the topic of this book is the role that MLE plays in facilitating a transfer of that which is learned (the specific content) through cognitive skills that enable the relating and elaborating of what is learned to other areas of functioning.

Throughout this book, the author describes situations of learning from a cognitive perspective—the *how* to learn—and the relevant relationships to the content—the *what* to learn. We believe that this process is an essential aspect of meaningful, adaptive, and sustained learning. To illustrate this process we propose the following metaphor:

> There are two shores on the sides of a flowing river. The flowing river represents consciousness and awareness that accompanies a dual process: learning the thinking and applying it to different contexts. On the right shore the student is exposed to teaching, mediation, and develops a repertoire of skills, insights, and cognitive structures and strategies for thinking. On the left shore is the plethora of facts, details, specific instances, and information that are available to encounter. The learning on the right shore, developing strategies, overcoming and/or strengthening any deficient or fragile cognitive functions, then is "bridged over" to the left shore and used to address the domain of content. The learned content is thus solidified, organized, grouped, and understood in a deeper and more abstracted (rules, principles, applications, etc.) way.

In the FIE program, we call this process *bridging*, and build it into the structure of the lesson. In this process, the cognitive structures that are learned in the FIE lesson are bridged over to the content. If we teach well the processes of learning, with flexibility and insightfulness (learning the rules, formulae, general applications, etc.) we will find that the bridging to content becomes transformative, and the student approaches new content with a flexibility and awareness that goes far beyond the specific instance or encounter.

There is, however, another basis for the consonance between our theoretical and practical approach—that of cognitive modifiability—and the development of the approach to teaching and learning that is reflected in this volume. It is the role of need and belief in our response to the needs of the many children and families about whom we share concerns. While it is clear that the child with learning difficulties and their families, teachers, and the communities in which they live have *needs*, I am referring to *our need* as teachers, parents, and therapists to respond to them. I have formulated this in the following way:

> The need creates a belief, and the belief leads to the search for ways to materialize that belief.

If we need to have children succeed, we cannot let the child fail. Our need will generate a belief that what we need to have happen is achievable. With this belief, we will search for ways to help the child learn, we will take responsibility, fight for options, not give up, and encourage, stimulate, push, and prod those who are in a position to help, and ultimately we will succeed. We will bring ingenuity, creativity, persistence, and an enduring faith that our belief will be materialized. We will search for the best methods and explore all options to confirm our belief. This was our experience with the thousands of children who survived the Holocaust and needed to be integrated into the society of Israel who gathered them in. It should be the response to all those students who are not learning, who are not fulfilling their potential, but can be helped and brought back into the educational structures and can take their ultimate place in society that their real talent and potential is suited for. Those of us who have had this experience, including the author of this book, know what "miracles" can be accomplished. That it feels so for the students who are helped, for their families and teachers, is testament to the power of the need and the belief, and all that flows from it.

In this sense, this book thus represents a very successful attempt to translate our theory of SCM, the new knowledge of the plasticity of the brain, and an awareness of the demands of modern society into practice. It does so in straight-forward and accessible ways. Returning to the NILD roots that we see in this approach, and the success of the movement to infuse educational interventions with cognitive and mediational components, it is to the honor of the movement that it looks to understand why it succeeds and to continue to look for ways to improve outcomes. In this regard, it is my view that this book makes a major contribution.

October 2009

Professor Reuven Feuerstein
Founder and Director
International Center for the Enhancement of Learning Potential
Jerusalem, Israel

INTRODUCTION

From my earliest school experiences I dreamed of becoming a teacher. Today, as a teacher of teachers, the fulfillment of my dreams has exceeded my expectations. To write a book for teachers is my "skylight."

I have borrowed from Oliver Wendell Holmes Sr. the idea of the three-story intellect with "skylights" as a frame of reference for the ideas I present in this book. My original intent was to put tools into teachers' hands to facilitate the teaching of *how to learn* in a *what-to-learn* culture. But my passion to see teachers grow in both competence and confidence and to find their own skylights returns again and again. I find I can't leave it alone. So while I trust students will benefit from the many suggestions and ideas included here, this book is primarily for teachers, encouraging and affirming their professional and cognitive growth.

My colleagues around the world are under new pressures to perform in a global race for educational excellence. I have watched some fine ones fall. It is my strong conviction that teachers need more than just a pat on the back and yet one more new idea to try. They need to know that they are competent to teach.

The ideas presented here are challenging. I have not proposed easy solutions to the educational dilemmas in which we find ourselves. But I have placed great confidence in our teachers and prescribed a way through the plethora of time limitations and endless worksheets that seem to be defining our rush to confirm our instructional success.

The premise of the book is that oral language directs and supports thinking skills. These are not new ideas. I have drawn on the theories of Piaget, Vygotsky, and Feuerstein and their ideas of cognitive modifiability and mediated learning. Through their collective genius I have devised practical suggestions for teachers to use with their students while, in the process, becoming cognitively changed themselves. Each chapter builds on the preceding one, so it is helpful to read them sequentially.

This is a book about learning how to learn, a process that never really stops for any of us. But it is also about the great adventure of meeting a child in the midst of a struggle and having the professional confidence and competence to get through the struggle and reach a skylight.

The great good news for educators, it seems to me, is that both students and teachers can increase their abilities to learn. There is no ceiling, ever. Learning how to capitalize on this great news is what most of the book is about. It is written for all teachers at all grade levels. My hope is that in addition to middle and elementary teachers, many high school teachers will see its relevance in their content-driven domains.

I have selected Aesop's fables to illustrate life principles for today's youth. The time line of educational principles reaches back through the centuries. I have also woven my own story into each chapter. It tells of both triumph and defeat, part of every teacher's story.

Ultimately, I have written *Teaching How to Learn in a What-to-Learn Culture* to inspire change, to restore a sense of adventure, and to fill weary teachers' toolboxes with some fresh ideas. It requires a certain openness to try new things, a willingness to put aside some things that do not work, and above all a strong belief in the resiliency and propensity of the human spirit. My sincere hope is that you will close the book with a strong sense of "I can do this!" Happy reading.

TEACHING
HOW TO LEARN
IN A WHAT-TO-LEARN
CULTURE

CHAPTER ONE

THE INTELLIGENCE DILEMMA

"I don't want to have the territory of a man's mind fenced in. . . . Their best illumination comes from above, through the skylight."
OLIVER WENDELL HOLMES SR.

I CAN REMEMBER, as a child, seeing a skylight for the first time. The ability to see clouds and blue sky through the roof gave me a thrilling sense of delight. It meant the ceiling did not have the last word. It meant endless possibilities, imagination, vision, dreams. Today, as an educator, I have several skylights in my home that continue to remind me of a world in which there are no limits, only possibilities. That is what this book is about.

As teachers we operate in a world of limits. There are time lines, deadlines, tests that have ceilings, students who have limitations. We desperately need to find the skylights. What exactly are these windows in the roof in relation to our noble profession? I will try to build the case that skylights relate to thinking, learning, assessment, and intelligence.

OPENING THE SKYLIGHT

We underrate our brains and our intelligence. Formal education has become such a complicated and overregulated activity that learning is widely regarded as something difficult that the brain would rather not do. Is it possible that the brain yearns to learn and that good teaching can actually improve the way the brain functions? This is the idea that the skylight represents. This opening in the ceiling implies a lifting of restrictions, unimagined possibilities, a transcending of the predictable. So what do I mean by intelligence?

Intelligence may be best described as an abstract concept, such as beauty or honesty, rather than one that is concrete. The attributes beauty and honesty are measurable, but with greater or lesser objectivity, depending on who is doing the evaluating. And it is certainly agreed that these attributes can change over time. So it is with intelligence.

Intelligence, I would argue, is not a concrete thing, like a house or an egg crate composed of rooms or cells. Nor is it a *trait* of an individual—such as blue eyes—that cannot be changed. Intelligence is better viewed as a *state* that is fully able to be changed under the right conditions (Feuerstein, 2007).

A more complete and compelling definition of intelligence for our purposes as educators is this (Feuerstein, 2002):

> **Intelligence is more correctly defined as the continuous changing state of a person best reflected in the way that individual is able to use previous experiences to adapt to new situations.**

The concept is in fact summed up by the words *the ability to learn from what has been learned.* This propensity for flexibility and dynamic unpredictability is within every learner. This assurance that each individual has the propensity for change becomes the real joy of teaching. In fact, believing in these new possibilities can help us adjust what might be an outdated concept in our own thinking—that intellectual potential is static, unchanging. Let's begin to unwrap some new concepts.

A CONCEPTUAL UNDERSTANDING OF INTELLIGENCE

We hear a lot about intelligence these days. Is it an important concept? What should we as teachers understand about it? Definitions of intelligence are controversial. We have certain beliefs based on prior experience that must be challenged in light of emerging knowledge in the fields of education and psychology. Let's take a closer look.

If I asked you to rate yourself as above average, average, or below the norm in intellectual functioning, where would you place yourself? This is an important question. It has been said that teachers are the most fragile of professionals, often regarding their own intellectual competency as low to moderate. Examining your personal assumptions about intelligence may remove some misconceptions and provide new ways of thinking about yourself and your students.

Our beliefs guide our practice. It is necessary to examine our beliefs about our students, ourselves, and yes, even our own capabilities in light of current theories and research. As we dig a bit deeper into the theories, perhaps we will discover that we and our students are more intelligent than we ever dreamed. Let's probe new insights and explore together the meaning of *intellectual propensity.* Hang in with me here. We are going to set the stage for some amazing discoveries. My strong conviction is that you will not be the same teacher when we have finished our journey together.

DEFINING INTELLIGENCE

How many times have you used the word *smart* to describe students in your classrooms, wondering if they might be just a bit smarter than you or at least may become so sooner than you would like? What do we mean by *smart?* Does it mean intelligent, witty, creative, or just clever? It may well be just the ability to adapt to one's environment as in *street smart.* Does *smart* mean the same thing as *intelligent? Cleverness* may refer to the ability to cleverly adapt to changing circumstances. There seem to be great differences in interpretation among all these words.

There is little consensus among professionals on an operative definition of intelligence. For example, when two dozen prominent theorists from the American Psychological Association were asked to define intelligence, they gave two dozen different definitions (1995). The concept is wide open to interpretation. We who are educators should understand some basics. For the sake of the intellectual rigor that upholds our profession, let's explore the intelligence dilemma together and examine three prominent theories explained by Rafi Feuerstein (1997).

Theory One: Cast Building

It has long been held that there is a measurable general intelligence factor common to all people. Intelligence quotients (IQ's) have been widely used in educational, business, and military settings. This first theory assumes that there is one basic factor responsible for thinking, or a general mental energy known as "g." This one factor "g" is presumed to be related to all thinking abilities. Because of its rigidity, this theory could be referred to as "cast building," as in building a concrete wall. Intelligence is seen as a global capability that causes an individual to respond similarly in all situations, or to all concepts or ideas. Those holding to this theory conclude that intellectual capacity is a relatively easy thing to measure and one that remains fairly consistent across an individual's lifetime. Is this your belief?

Theory Two: Brick Building

A second theory is a bit more flexible. Rather than *cast building,* it could be described as *brick building.* This theory refers to intelligence that has a number of factors responsible for various thinking abilities, and these factors are separate from one another, like bricks in a wall. Separation is due to the content involved in the thinking processes, as in Gardner's (1993) multiple intelligences theory. This separation of process and content implies different ways of thinking relative to different subject areas. For example, you may have a spatial intelligence that helps you design buildings and find your way in a strange city but not be able to read very well.

A problem, according to Feuerstein, in considering intellectual ability as separate areas, or "bricks," is that one area of intellectual competence presumably has nothing to do with any other areas of cognitive strength or weakness. That is, this second theory presumes that the systems that support the ability to design a building or read a book have no overlap. Nevertheless, it does introduce some flexibility into the intelligence dilemma.

Have you landed on a specific position yet? Can you be supersmart in one area and really dumb in another? Or are there supporting systems such as flexibility of thinking that underlie both?

Theory Three: Mosaic Model

A third theory could be called the *mosaic model*. This model resembles a colorful, creatively designed mosaic tile as opposed to a concrete or brick wall. The theory is more flexible than the cast building theory and more general than the brick building one. The mosaic model integrates the features of the other two by proposing:

- Intelligence is built from many factors within an individual, both cognitive and experiential.

- These many factors are general and can be related to all cognitive behaviors (like designing or reading).

- Intelligence can be described as either fluid or crystallized (Cattell, 1987).

You could picture fluid intelligence as being the background on which the mosaic tiles are placed. Fluid intelligence consists of thinking strategies that are separate from the content being learned. In other words, it is *how* one thinks, not *what*. Crystallized intelligence, in contrast, is the specific knowledge learned by the individual or the content or body of knowledge that the individual has mastered. It is the mosaic tiles themselves that represent functional cognitive systems.

In other words, this theory assumes intelligence that is separate from the knowledge learned or content measured by many IQ tests. Fluid intelligence— the how to learn—can cross over into many content areas and is open to constructive change. For example, strengthening visual processing could contribute to greater fluency in reading, thereby improving comprehension skills. In fact, improvement in fluid intelligence can contribute to content mastery or crystallization of knowledge. This is great news for all educators. It means that limits that were previously set now have a skylight—a window in the ceiling formerly imposed by intelligence predictions.

Let's return to our skylight analogy. According to Holmes (1993), there are one-story intellects, two-story intellects, and three-story intellects with skylights. Those who only collect facts are one-story individuals. Two-story individuals compare, reason, and generalize, based on the facts of the fact collectors. Three-story individuals idealize, imagine, and predict. Their best illumination comes from above, through the skylight. If we can begin to understand that intelligence is wonderfully open to change throughout a lifetime and that, as teachers, we can influence intellectual development though our teaching, then the *how* to learn will take new priority over the *what*.

In one sentence, write what you believe about intelligence.

Now, apply your belief to your own intelligence and the way you function cognitively. Do you think the *way in which you learn* has an impact on *what* you learn or master? In other words, does your fluid intelligence, your basic cognitive functioning, provide for the acquisition of knowledge?

Let's take an example. Suppose you are having difficulty finding your way in a strange town. You have a map but cannot seem to orient yourself to the street directions. In fact, you are confused about left and right. Based on past experience, you know that stopping to ask for directions may confuse you even more. Then you remember a strategy to deal with this problem. You stop the car and turn the map in the direction that you are traveling. All turns then can be handled easily, because you have oriented yourself in space.

This same remedy, reorienting either yourself or the material, can apply in other contexts. This is an example of fluid intelligence because it crosses categories. In other words, the correct orientation of visual information is useful in other tasks, such as reading, regardless of their content. If good teaching can contribute to structural changes in fluid intelligence, then the content to be learned will become crystallized more easily whatever the subject area.

Are you with me so far? We will add meat to these bones in succeeding chapters.

Let's get practical for a moment. All theories must be tested in the classroom. Engage students in an activity that will affect fluid intelligence in the realm of visual processing.

CLASSROOM ACTIVITY

First, copy a series of pictures onto a transparency.

- Tell students you are going to show them the series for five seconds and they are to remember the pictures in that order. Then you will show them the same pictures but in a different order with numbers under them. Your students must put the pictures back into the order of the first transparency.

- Project the first set of pictures on the screen, hold for five seconds (or more if you sense they need it).

- Give a few seconds for processing, then put up the second set of the pictures, which are now in a different order. Have your students write the pictures' numbers on their papers in the order in which they first appeared.

- Discuss strategies to use for remembering. This is the most important part of the activity. Some may say they made a sentence to remember. Some will say they just kept saying them over and over. Some will have tried to remember just by their using their visual memory. But all should understand the importance of giving the pictures a label (that is, naming the picture mentally: moose, ball, clock, and so on).

Language is key to making connections; it is the DNA of fluid intelligence. If we can improve language, both inner and spoken, then we can affect intellectual functioning. This activity not only builds processing skills through strengthening visual memory but also contributes to strategic thinking and fluid intelligence, the *how* to learn. Let's continue to explore the intelligence dilemma.

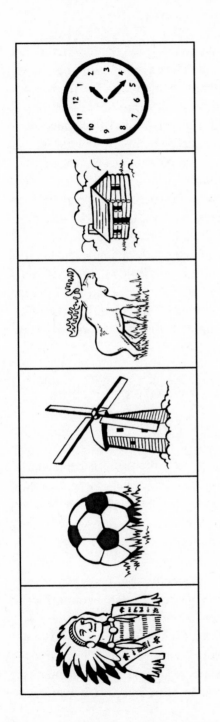

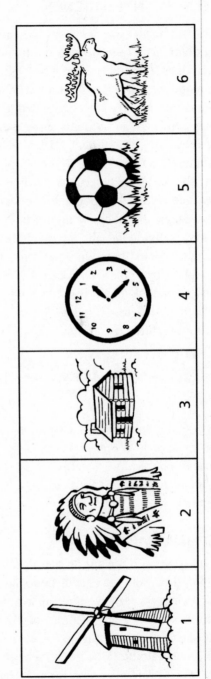

FIGURE 1.1. Visual Memory Stimulation

THE ROOT OF INTELLIGENCE

To define intelligence we must first consider the theories and the research done by the individuals who proposed the theories. We have already examined three prominent ones. In addition, the word itself should be analyzed. The root of the word intelligence is *intellegere*, Latin for "to understand." *Intelligence* implies a general mental capacity that varies from person to person and fluctuates over a lifespan. Different individuals have particular propensities or deficits in the areas of reasoning, planning, problem solving, comprehending abstract ideas, and learning from experience. Innate abilities or disabilities in these areas, however, should never be seen as permanent or unmodifiable. All learners can improve their ability to recognize connections as well as develop the capacity to think strategically, thereby laying the groundwork for new knowledge.

Clearly, individuals vary in their ability to understand complex ideas, to adapt effectively to their environments, to engage in different kinds of reasoning, and to overcome obstacles by creative thought. In addition, a given individual's intellectual performance will vary greatly on any given day and when judged by different criteria. Here is one simple definition that incorporates many of the qualities mentioned:

Intelligence is the ability to recognize and make connections.

This simple definition is extremely relevant to us as we explore learning how to learn in a classroom setting. It may even represent a benchmark for you and your students. How well do you recognize and make connections? Can you teach this skill to your students to enhance their intellectual competency?

Intellectual Potential?

If you ever took an IQ test, you were placed in a category that perhaps "boxed you in" for life. You may have believed that your intellectual potential was measured, when actually your score was merely a predictor of how well you would do in school. The inventors of IQ tests reportedly never believed they were measuring fixed intelligence, yet in practice many educators have translated the scores into biological realities that can never change. Binet, the author of one of the first intelligence tests, is reported to have said, "If it were not possible to change intelligence, why measure it in the first place?" (cited in Campioni, 1989, p. 155).

For example, one look at a child with Down's syndrome assures many that any attempt to improve on this child's intellectual functioning would be futile. Yet how many enlightened teachers would declare, "Chromosomes do not have the last word" (Feuerstein, 2006). Many children who have Down's syndrome today are achieving far more than anyone believed they could fifty years ago. Perhaps the most important quality of intelligence that Feuerstein's mosaic theory presents is *modifiability*—that is, the belief that intelligence is not constant or static, but wonderfully open to constructive change for all learners throughout a lifetime.

Mediated Learning

As we enter the arena of intellectual dynamic unpredictability, or the realization that learning is not a lockstep, highly predictable process, we learn to expect change in our students. Embracing the "mosaic model" means that the teacher should believe in the reversibility of poor academic performance, not doubt it. Intellectual skills can be developed by both teachers and students. However, such change does not happen by chance or without understanding the mediator's role in the process.

STOPANDTHINK

Do you believe good teaching can actually change the intellectual capacity of a child?

The good news for teachers is that all minds can be stretched, inherent abilities unmasked, and thought processes developed—even our own! The secret lies in unwrapping the amazing concept of *mediated learning*. Mediated learning, in brief, relies on the guidance of an adult, whose role is to help interpret the complex world of input from the environment so that the child can focus, frame, and consider relationships. An extra bonus is that in the process of teaching a child to learn, the teacher too becomes better able to learn and think and make those all important connections. We will discuss mediated learning in more detail in the next chapter.

LET'S GET PERSONAL

Consider your classroom:

- Do you see your students in categories?

- Are the bright ones in the front row (literally or figuratively)?

- In contrast, are the slower ones in the back?

- What about those average learners? You may be really surprised to learn that some in the back row actually have an ability to think more abstractly and make more meaningful connections than those who succeed so well in memorizing the school subjects.

Consider your teaching style:

- Do you tend to lower your expectations to a student's current level of functioning?

- Do you call on the first hand that is up to keep the lesson moving?

- Do you do most of the talking during a school day? Do you consider memorization the goal for mastery of a concept?

Consider your personal level of confidence and competence:

- Do you think you are a good teacher?

- Are you confident that all students in your class are learning?

- Do you give preferential treatment to the bright students who learn easily?

- Are struggling learners a chore or a welcome challenge?

- Do you believe your own thinking and learning are modifiable?

STOPANDTHINK

Discuss these questions with a colleague. Reflect on your beliefs about thinking and learning. They are deeply imbedded. Be open to some new ideas.

As we confront the very roots of our beliefs about ability and intelligence let's recall our first school experiences. This is my story.

STARTING SCHOOL

The year was 1949, and my father had just received military orders to Lakenheath Air Force Base in central England following World War II. Postwar England was a sad and dreary place. It seemed the hearts of the people had been damaged beyond the devastation of the countryside. Ration cards restricted the purchase of many staples, including sugar, butter, and eggs. The war had taken a terrible toll on the country. When we arrived there from America, we could feel the misery. We had come to help.

From my five-year-old perspective, the long, dark days, damp woolen uniforms, meager rations, and never-ending split pea soup for lunch had only a minimal negative impact on my first school experiences. For *I was going to school,* an event I had yearned for since my earliest memories. I was, as my mother said, "wired for it." From the first I was clamorous to learn and could hardly contain the wonder of books and desks and teachers.

I began my formal schooling in a very strict parochial school in a little village called Bury St. Edmonds. The nuns were unbending in their discipline. There was certainly no foolishness allowed and definitely no fun. I have few memories of lessons learned or favorite teachers, yet it was here, I believe, that my desire to become a teacher was formed. Maybe it had something to do with the discipline and work ethic or the childlike wonder of learning for its own sake without the frills. Learning to read was one of my greatest joys because it opened to my curious mind whole new worlds. My natural quest for adventure found an outlet in learning, and I soaked it in like a sponge.

However, my curiosity and adventurous spirit got the better of me one day when I climbed up on the altar in the church to see if Jesus really was under that draped chalice as the nuns said he was. I did not see him. Even the severe discipline of Sister Paul Mary did not deter my quest for knowledge. Was I intelligent? I think intellectually curious would be a better description. In any case, my first three years of schooling in England set me on a course of learning for life and helped form many of my beliefs about education. The formation of my intellectual curiosity happened despite the hardships. I did not need worksheets, colorful pages, stars for performance, or grades that affirmed my competence. I had an innate joy in learning for its own sake. As I reflect on the model of the three-story intellect, I see that I yearned for more than just the facts. Staying on the first floor held no appeal. I wanted the skylight.

Reflect for a moment on your early school experiences. Those events helped shape your perceptions of your abilities and aptitudes. They define for you the beginning understandings of your intellectual abilities, your desire to learn, and your attitudes toward other learners. In fact, they may help explain why you became a teacher. As educators, it is helpful for us to examine the circumstances of our lives that led us into this profession. Each of us comes to it with a belief system shaped through personal experiences.

Take a moment to jot down or discuss your own early educational experiences with a spouse or friend and discuss what you believe today about teaching and learning because of those early experiences.

Some, like me, became teachers because they found learning to be an adventure and wanted to experience every bit of it. Others found learning difficult and became teachers to try to change the system that was so frustrating for them. Still others followed the profession of their parents. For many, the "call" to teach was loud and clear, sometimes coming in spite of a strong desire *not* to be an educator. Perhaps the motivation for some was proving to others that they *could* teach.

Parents play a strategic role in shaping our beliefs about our own intelligence. We are often compared, positively or negatively, to siblings. In fact, these beliefs generally stay with us throughout our lifetimes. A simple statement such as "You must have been last in line when the brains were handed out" can relegate us to the back row not just in school but in any intellectual pursuit. By the same token, hearing how smart we are can be a positive reinforcement. An important question is how smart you feel or think you are today. Has anything changed for you from those early childhood beliefs?

I hope that by now you are beginning to challenge the concept that intelligence is fixed from birth. It is time to put to rest the idea that intellectual capacity is determined by genetics and therefore unchangeable. Instead, try to picture a continuum of propensity—an openness to change—that develops over a lifetime. Now, see the linear continuum rise into a trajectory of ever-increasing abilities. This is your legacy and mine. More importantly, it must be transmitted to the students we teach. Both competence and confidence can be powerfully enhanced. It all begins with what you, the teacher, believe about thinking and learning. For, as I will share later, I was not the most brilliant bulb in the box! My own journey to intellectual competence took many turns in the road.

PRACTICAL APPLICATION

Let's bring our theory into classroom practice. For in order to make an impact on fluid intelligence through our teaching, we must learn how. I have chosen to use the fables of Aesop (Ashliman, 2003) throughout this book to illustrate "how-to-learn" principles. These stories are oral traditions handed down to us through many generations. The mind of man seeks instruction and delights in telling stories that illustrate life principles. Fables, proverbs, and riddles are meant to inspire intellectual curiosity and draw us into their challenges. I hope you will see that these fables' principles can apply to any grade level or subject matter and interface with any curriculum.

The First Fable

The Frogs and the Well

 Two frogs lived together in a marsh. But one hot summer the marsh dried up, and they left it to look for another place to live, for frogs like damp places if they can get them. By and by they came to a deep well, and one of them looked down into it and said to the other, "This looks like a nice cool place.

Let us jump in and settle here." But the other who had a wiser head on his shoulders, replied, "Not so fast, my friend. Supposing this well dried up like the marsh; how shall we get out again?"

This tale is brimming with intelligence-enhancing opportunities. Specifically, let's apply the three theories of intelligence in this chapter to the fable in order to crystallize them for you. Let's first think of the cast building theory or the *g* factor. In this model a teacher would have different expectations for responses from her students, having already mentally assigned them to "groups." Therefore, following the introduction of this fable, she would ask the easier questions to the lower group and the more complex questions to the higher group. A teacher who subscribed to the brick building theory would teach to the specific learning styles of the students. She might have the artists in her class visualize the scene and the kinesthetic learners construct it. A teacher who understood the mosaic theory would assume that all learners could achieve a high level of abstraction in deciding the meaning of the fable while building connections to past experiences, as illustrated in the following paragraphs.

Let's assume you have used this fable in a reading lesson or as part of a science or history unit. You could project the text on the wall for whole-class viewing, then develop some specific questions to promote class involvement.

Prepare the Lesson

But before revealing the text on the screen ask, "Jan, what do you know about frogs?" Don't wait for a hand; ask a specific student and then another. "Ed, do you have more you could add?" "Can you share a personal experience you have had with a frog?" "Describe a frog. In what scientific category could you put a frog? Why? What else would go in that category? What would not?" Explore knowledge through oral language. You are helping students make connections through your questioning.

Project the Text of the Fable

After projecting the text ask, "What do you see here?" Many will want to get right into the content, but focus them with a question such as, "Can you describe the page?" Enlist the response, "A title and a short paragraph." Ask, "Is the author listed?" "Do you think you might know who the author is?" Aesop should be part of a student's vocabulary of cultural literacy. Then, "What is a fable?" Lead students by helping them restate their answers to reach a clear, concise definition. Check a dictionary prior to the lesson for clear, specific terminology.

Depending on your class, have the passage read silently or orally and then begin a group discussion on what lesson the fable teaches. You may need to provide some hints. As a class, see if you can come up with ideas. Some examples might be:

- Look before you leap.
- Haste makes waste.
- Think before you rush into something new.

Build Intelligence

Select one of the options and write it on the board after developing it collaboratively as a whole group. This is high-level abstract reasoning. Getting students to talk about the lesson of the fable challenges them to stretch their intellectual powers. And yours. Tell them that.

Ask: "What does this passage teach us about intelligence? How intelligent was the first frog? The second? Were they both able to learn from past experiences? What behavior of the second frog made you think he was intelligent? Can you think of an example from your own life when you were doing something similar to what the frogs did?" Be prepared to share an example from your childhood experience. Students love to hear your stories. This personalization of the fable stretches the learning into a different context, developing cognitive strengths that transfer to other learning.

These suggestions are specifically designed to build intellectual competency, and because they are intended to be answered orally by students, they have the power to direct meaningful thought processes. The power of oral language will be explored later.

Develop Cognitive Competence

As you probe student thinking through open-ended questions, you will begin to see new cognitive skills emerge. Connecting to students' prior experience is always a great place to start. Engage them immediately with what they already know or have personally experienced. Keep the dialogue fun, light, and entertaining. This is a great time for you to share your frog experiences!

Having your students describe the layout or format of the page in clear and precise language helps direct efficient thinking processes and evolves into the great skill of being able to predict tasks by the layout of the page, even before reading the directions. When students begin to anticipate the task based on the page format, it means they are being trained in observation skills that will eventually become internalized and automatic. So, for any new task begin with the question, "What do you see on this page?" Work toward a clear, succinct verbal response. For example: "There are no blanks on this page and no explicit instructions, so I am going to have to infer some things based on the content of the paragraph."

The ability to put words into categories is an important cognitive skill. Noting likenesses and differences refines intellectual and verbal abilities. In addition, students benefit greatly by hearing their peers express their knowledge.

Even more intellectually challenging is the ability to summarize and state a lesson the fable teaches. Have your students work in pairs in future sessions to encourage oral exploration of possibilities. Select a sentence and write it on the board to crystallize the activity. For example, you or a student may write:

Being intelligent and wise means being able to think both backwards to what happened before and forward to what might happen.

Again, the skill of a master teacher in the learning process provides the structure your students need to direct their own learning. Through your questioning, you are teaching them how to learn. Then the "what," or content, will come more easily. You are building fluid, intellectual competence.

As you purpose to raise your expectations above your students' actual levels of performance, you will be amazed at the hidden propensities that emerge. Begin by:

- Engaging the quiet ones
- Not calling on the first hand you see
- Moving strategically around the room
- Helping students restate their weak verbal responses
- Being one of the learners
- Setting appropriate challenges

- Modeling your own love of learning
- Building respect for all sincere responses.

REFLECTION

We have begun to infuse some new ideas into the intelligence dilemma. Are you beginning to wonder in your mind and heart if in your classroom in this year you might actually be able to change your students' abilities to think, reason, remember, and reflect? And to do the same with your own? As teachers, we are not called to simply build fact upon fact; instead, we have the great privilege of renovating the mind's architecture—in particular, constructing a skylight, a window in those man-made ceilings.

Teaching is both art and science. As you become more confident and competent in your ability to get students talking in meaningful ways to you and to each other, you will begin to equip them with tools that will keep getting better and better. The secret will be unwrapped in the concepts of *cognitive modifiability* and *mediated learning*. We will examine both in the next chapter.

CHAPTER TWO

A WAY OUT OF THE PRESSURE COOKER

"Learning stamps you with its moments. Childhood's learning is made of moments. It is not steady. It is a pulse."

EUDORA WELTY, *ONE WRITER'S BEGINNINGS*

A NEW LIFE

In 1952, my family returned from England to the United States, where I was eager to begin fourth grade in the small town of Bridgeville, Delaware (population 3,500). My father was now out of the military and had returned to his hometown to help my grandfather on the family farm. It was Labor Day, and the roadside market that they ran was particularly busy, so I was amusing myself by playing on the tractor that was standing idle in the field. Before I knew what happened, I had slid from the smooth surface of the tractor's body where I was relaxing on my stomach and slammed hard onto the ground, breaking my arm in two places.

Being a very religious child (even though I had not seen Jesus under the drape at school in England!), I quickly ran up to the house, fell on my knees, and in a wild, tearful prayer asked God to help me! There was no immediate evidence of such assistance, but I marched bravely to the market and fearfully told my parents about my mishap. They were not too pleased to have to take me to the hospital that day, the busiest of the year. Looking back now, I know it was not a hard-hearted response but a fearful one. We were counting on the income from the sale of our produce.

The moments of my life surged like a pulse, and my memories of them shape me still. The idea of having to walk into a new school with a cast on my arm kept me awake and in tears the night before. Any sense of joy in going to school was quickly overshadowed by a deep insecurity and sadness because of my accident. Would I be laughed at or teased? I was a year younger and smaller than my peers, having begun school in England at the age of four, and that made me even more vulnerable.

So I began fourth grade with a cast on my right arm, forcing me to write with my left. This seemed to place me in a very precarious academic position. I not only had to adjust to a very different school culture than the one I had just left but also spoke with a peculiar English accent, and my handwriting looked like I had subnormal intelligence. My teacher, Miss Scott, had certain very proper ways of running a classroom, and never having encountered a child who had been schooled in England before, was not quite sure what to do with me. In the end, I was given an F in handwriting, and was sent off to the fifth grade in the hopes I could do better.

In addition to these humbling experiences, my father and mother were going through the postwar stresses that many families had in those days, so life at home became quite noisy and argumentative. I withdrew more and more into a private world that I could order, and I brought my younger brother, Jackie, along with me. On one memorable occasion, there was a fierce argument going on in the kitchen, then a terrific bang. The pressure cooker had exploded and pieces of macaroni hung everywhere. Jackie and I looked on in wonder as Mom and Dad trembled at their good fortune that the lid, which had made a great hole in the ceiling, had not fallen on their heads!

THE PRESSURES ARE REAL

In reality, many in school settings today feel the pressure of the "cooker." We are in a global race, and our educational systems are under scrutiny by the rest of the world. America has always been its own worst critic, and our perceptions of our fragile educational system have fired international criticism. Our global "standings" have taken on political ramifications, resulting in demoralized teachers and forcing many to leave this time-honored profession. Some teachers have recently made these comments:

> **"I am retiring early primarily due to the manner in which I am forced to teach and assess."**
> **"I don't teach much reading anymore: I am too busy testing children."**
> **"We feel we are fleeing a sinking ship, after giving our entire lives to our students and our profession."**
> **"It is a sad way to end a career."**

The pressures have invaded the classrooms and challenged the status quo. Both methods and methodologies are in question, so that teacher confidence and competence have suffered. As the rest of the world looks on, the internal pressures to perform continue to build.

Yet America still leads the world in two important qualities formed in the schools of our nation: creativity and innovation. I was recently on a train in India sitting opposite two professors from South Korea. In our conversation, they remarked that most foreign students long to attend American universities simply because they encourage student debate, are open to fresh new ideas, and are not overly focused on test scores. If this is true at the university level, an important question to be asked is, "What is happening in our elementary and secondary schools?"

Innovation, a blending of intellect and imagination, has truly catapulted and sustained America's place as a dominant economic force in the global economy. But China and India are on the move in the areas of technology and manufacturing. A great book that explains this phenomenon is *The Elephant and the Dragon* by Robyn Meredith (2007). China is turning out an abundance of engineers, and India is excelling in technology. But the Chinese themselves have noted that no one from their country has yet won the Nobel Prize. If we downplay innovation and creative thinking at the expense of performing well on standardized tests, we will not only lose our creative teachers but also lose our credibility as a superpower.

Reflect for a moment on this quote (Caine and Caine, 1991):

"Meaningful learning is essentially creative. All students must be given permission to transcend the insights of their teachers."

LET'S GET PERSONAL

Have you sensed rising pressure and stress as you prepare students for tests? It is important to remember that test-taking has always been a stress producer for students and teachers alike. I expect that back in 1952 my teacher, Miss Scott, stressed out on testing days.

A SURVEY

Consider changes that you have had to make in your classroom to accommodate mandatory testing.

- What aspects of these changes have been helpful to you and your students?

- What aspects have been difficult?

It may be helpful to make a list of the pros and cons of the new testing requirements; there will likely be some of both. Then compare your list with a colleague's.

- Do you agree that there is certain content information that forms the body of cultural literacy necessary for all to know who live in the United States or in any given culture?

- Do you think today's focus on content knowledge is helpful in building a stronger base of informed literacy for all students?

- Do you feel that the way you are now teaching contributes to increased intellectual curiosity in your students?

- Are you able to lead them into the pure joy of learning for its own sake and not simply to perform well on a test?

Finally, think about your own situation.

- When was the last time you personally learned something new just for the fun of it?

- Has your love of learning increased or diminished over the past years? Can you identify the causes?

Reflect again on your early schooling when you were gaining information by reading in various subject areas. What sparked your interest or made you want to know more? Did you have any difficulty reading for information? Nothing derails intellectual curiosity more thoroughly than a reading problem. If you did not struggle with reading difficulties, how did you feel about those who did? Our attitudes toward those who have educational challenges are usually formed in elementary school. The challenge of struggling learners remains very much with us today. Does their lack of progress fuel frustration for you?

Identify the Pressures

The first step in getting out of the cooker is to take inventory of the pressures you are facing. What are they? I am going to suggest a list, and you decide whether you experience these specific pressures.

- Many students are struggling in the classroom and cannot seem to learn no matter how many ways I try to present the material.

- Behavior problems seem to trump instruction, and I spend my time trying to keep order rather than teaching.

- It seems I am always teaching to the next test rather than actually teaching children.

- There is too wide a gap in learner ability in my classroom, so I am teaching to the middle and leaving out the brightest and the slowest.

- There is such competition for scores that my colleagues guard their trade secrets so that there is little sharing of professional knowledge.

- The administrators are not connected to the real issues in the classroom and have little sympathy for our complaints.

- I feel very alone in my job and wonder often if I am in the wrong profession.

You may have found that you identify with more than one of these pressure-cooker issues. Any one of them could cause significant stress, leading you to wonder if an explosion is imminent. Thankfully, there are answers. I will address many of these issues in the pages of this book. Begin by being honest about the pressures you feel, and together let's explore some solutions.

Find the Way Out

Let's return to Aesop. As it turns out, his fables contain nuggets of wisdom that apply to many of life's pressures.

The Horse and the Groom

There was once a groom who used to spend long hours clipping and combing the horse of which he had charge, but who daily stole a portion of its allowance of oats and sold it for his own profit. The horse gradually got into worse and worse condition, and at last cried to the groom, "If you really want me to look sleek and well, you must comb me less and feed me more."

Interesting moral lessons may indeed be found here, but how do they apply to education? For those who feel they are in a virtual pressure cooker as they teach our nation's children, this fable offers some insights. Are we grooming the outside of the "horse" (our students) through polished performances on tests and neglecting the real "food" of fostering a love of learning? It might be interesting to discuss who is really profiting from the high-stakes testing promoted by our "what-to-learn" culture.

Without being cynical, it is appropriate for thinking educators to ask hard questions of those who form educational policy. In fact, it may be useful to share this fable at a faculty meeting, using the interactive method outlined in Chapter One. Meaningful dialogue goes a long way toward helping us find solutions. Take any one item from the preceding list and spend some time sharing the pressures you are feeling. Perhaps generating a corporate-style list of the pros and cons of high-stakes testing would be helpful. Raising academic standards does not have to mean increased pressure for teachers. Let's purpose to make meaning of the struggles.

THE NEED FOR MEANINGFULNESS

Behavioral approaches have predominated in education for over sixty years. Behaviorism, advanced by Skinner (1938), rests on the theory that rewards motivate effective learning and punishment deters slackers. Schools use rewards, such as good grades or passed tests, to promote successful learning.

However, behaviorist theories ignore the power and vitality within students—that is, their innate capacity to create meaning for themselves. If the goal is simply to pass the test, students look to others, such as teachers or more capable peers, to do their thinking for them. According to Caine, as long ago as 1991 we had an entire generation working for grades and tangible rewards. That has not changed in the years since Caine and Caine wrote that; it may even be worse today. Many students have become unmotivated to seek answers for themselves and therefore are deprived of the joy of personal discovery. That same loss of joy affects teachers.

Piaget (1959) believed that children even from infancy were continually engaged in making sense of things. Truly, we are more than machines responding only to "information in, information out." Thinking educators understand that the teacher's role is not simply to put "information in" to students. Rather, teaching is the amazing privilege of allowing learners the wonder of discovering for themselves. How can we do this when we have so much information to cover? Many educational theorists agree that the human brain is at its best when it is thinking creatively. But let's be honest. Are we a bit afraid of creativity, preferring to stay within the dictates of the textbooks? Do you remember that dynamic unpredictability we discussed in Chapter One? Don't we prefer the predictable, the book with the answer keys? Let's dig a bit deeper into the knowledge dilemma. Clearly, knowledge can be acquired in different ways and for different reasons.

SURFACE VERSUS MEANINGFUL KNOWLEDGE

Surface knowledge may be described as anything that can be programmed into a computer (though our computers have become very clever!) or a robot. It is basically memorization of the mechanics of a subject. It aims for correct performance on a test. Meaningful knowledge, in contrast, is anything that makes sense to the learner.

There is increasing evidence that the brain responds very differently to surface knowledge as opposed to meaningful knowledge. For one thing, the brain strongly resists having meaningless information forced upon it. As Piaget believed, our brains are happiest when they are making meaning. Teachers' brains respond in the same way. We are happiest when we teach a subject we fully understand. Consider the subject that you do not really understand but have to teach anyway. Because you cannot make meaning from the subject, teaching it creates its own kind of pressure.

The search for meaning is at the very heart of motivation. Students must be inspired to wonder, develop intellectual curiosity, and desire to understand and find answers for themselves. We will talk more about the teacher's role in this adventure in the following chapters.

THE CASE FOR COGNITIVE MODIFIABILITY

So how do we tap into this gold mine of intrinsic motivation, assuming that it is lying dormant in the minds and hearts of our students? Keep in mind that memorization does have its place. It is a valuable tool in acquiring information and is often a prelude to understanding. But as we learned in the last chapter, intelligence is not fixed or static. It is dynamic, flexible, and resilient.

The principle of cognitive modifiability is one that every teacher should understand. When we press on to a deeper understanding of the pressures that face us, we can deal with them more successfully.

The wonderful thing about the mind is that it can be changed. This is also an unfortunate thing, for it can be either sharpened or dulled. Left alone or put with less able minds, it can slowly deteriorate. We know much about learning and thinking from a scientific standpoint because our technology has given us the ability to track the workings of the mind by observing the physical brain.

We have discussed that our experiences shape our minds. Quite possibly our social and educational experiences change the very structures of our brains, although this has yet to be proven scientifically. Dynamic, ever-changing fluid intelligence seems open to change throughout a person's lifetime. This, as I have said, is both good news and bad news.

Modifiability, or the ability to be changed at a deep, intellectual level, is a uniquely human characteristic. It goes beyond the stimulus-response behaviorism demonstrated by Pavlov's dogs. Many behaviorists consider biological factors the main if not the sole determinants in an individual's ability to learn and think.

Clearly, the genetic contribution to our abilities or disabilities is a strong one. However, it is not the only one. There is also the powerful force of human social interaction. Professor Reuven Feuerstein (2006) challenges the notion that the genome explains everything relative to brain functioning. His premise is that social-verbal interactions can moderate or change the power of the genome and lessen its influence on cognitive ability. What an amazing thought! It is my conviction that we would forever teach differently if we believed this. Some of the stressors on our list would be changed dramatically.

STOPANDTHINK

Have your perceptions of student potential caused you to adjust your expectations downward for struggling learners?

The biology of an individual does affect the way he responds to his environment. For example, a child who is hypersensitive, such as those who are severely autistic, resist touch. Yet there is strong evidence that the cultural environment into which a person is born has the power to change the biological factors. In other words, a sensitive, informed adult can, through specific intervention, gradually influence an autistic child to become less and less hypersensitive. This is the theory behind the statement, "Chromosomes do not have the last word." The human being can be described as the product of the constant, intense, and dynamic encounter between these two heredities, the biological and the sociocultural. But teachers must understand the role they play in the dynamic change process.

Cognitive modifiability refers to the *belief* that an individual can be changed structurally—that is, biologically—when a mediator (such as a teacher or parent) stands between the material to be learned and the student and helps to frame, focus, and filter the incoming information. Thus, mediated learning involves the purposeful and intentional positioning of an adult between the child and the stimulus in order to add meaning and relevance for the child. An example of mediated learning as opposed to direct exposure to stimuli follows.

> *Direct learning:* A young child touches the stove and is burned.
> *Mediated learning:* A mother takes her child's hand and gently brings it near the stove, saying, "Don't touch, hot."

Parents are a child's first mediators. They are the ones responsible for providing the guided experiences necessary for the child to benefit from a lifetime of learning; in fact, there is some evidence that a low level of mediation in the home can result in certain learning difficulties later in school (Feuerstein, 2007). Examples of effective mediation will be woven throughout this book.

The critical aspect of mediation is the constructive use of interactive language. Many busy parents today find it very difficult to mediate learning experiences. If they knew the power of the verbal exchanges, they might make time to interact verbally with their children in meaningful ways. However, even when there is no parental mediation, teachers can provide these opportunities during the school day. Let's explore some creative ways to apply the theories of cognitive modifiability and mediated learning in the classroom. Much depends on our ability to question and probe thinking.

PRACTICAL APPLICATIONS

It is the teacher's job to create a readiness to respond to teacher-directed questions by explaining the reasons why spoken language is important. As students understand the importance of oral language in directing thinking, there will be greater "buy-in" to become involved in dialogue. The tone can be set at the beginning of the year in the following way:

In our class this year, we are going to learn that our oral language is a very important tool to help direct our thinking processes. I will be asking you to

*explain what you are thinking or how you got your answer, and then I will help
you say what you said even better. I might say something like, "Could you use
another word for whatchamacallit in that sentence?" Or, "Could you give me
some more information?" We will work together on making sure our speech is
clear, brief, and to the point. It is my job to help you, but you must never feel
that I am trying to embarrass you or put you on the spot. By the end of the year
I predict we will all become better thinkers because we have worked hard on
making our speech say what we want it to.*

Take a look at your classroom. How is your room arranged? To facilitate
dialogue, students should be placed in small groups either at tables or with
desks facing one another. At the high school level, desks should be movable
to facilitate group work.

Let's look at a sample lesson that incorporates oral language and mediated learning. Teacher-directed questions often save time and get right into
the topic at hand. Waiting for a raised hand and then the recommended "wait
time" is not as productive as calling on a student directly as in the following
example:

TEACHER: John, what are the three R's of education?

STUDENT: Reading, writing, and 'rithmetic.

TEACHER: Great job using your long-term memory. This saying is part of
America's cultural literacy, so it is something you should know.
Abby, suppose I told you there was a fourth R. Can you think
for a moment and tell me what that might be?

STUDENT: I think it is racing, because that is what we seem to be doing
in school a lot, racing through our subjects.

TEACHER: Clever and funny thought, Abby. It does seem like that. Jill, do
you have an idea?

STUDENT: I thought of reasoning, because that is what Abby just did.

TEACHER: I am very impressed with *your* reasoning. Good thinking, Jill.
That is exactly what we are going to be talking about today.
Can you think of a good definition for reasoning? (Be sure to
look this up ahead of time and lead students to articulate a
clear, succinct definition.) *Reasoning: something that supports
a conclusion or explains a fact.*

Write it on the board after the students, with your mediation, together come up with a clear, concise meaning. Ask students when they have to use reasoning to solve a problem. Refer back to the previous dialogue. John *remembered* the three R's of education. That was a fact recalled from his long-term memory and did not really require reasoning. Both Abby and Jill were using their *reasoning* skills to think of a fourth R because that was something that they had never thought of before.

Ahead of time, select a page of text that you have recently been studying. Be sure it has high interest and captures your class's attention. A paragraph may be sufficient. For this task, *you* read the content with expression, modeling good oral language. Your students should follow along as you read.

After reading, have them orally generate questions that a test might ask about the material they just heard. Choose a scribe to record some of the questions on the board. Then have the class decide whether each question was a fact or a reasoning question by putting *F* (for fact) or *R* (for reasoning) next to each.

If no reasoning questions were generated, mediate (that is, frame or focus) by cueing your students to begin reasoning questions with "why" or "how." Have them decide and describe the differences between fact and reasoning. Mediate that these can be explained by the terms *surface knowledge* (memorization) and *meaningful knowledge* (understanding). When they can use these labels with understanding, you have helped generate new internal intellectual categories.

Then have students work in their groups to come up with a *great* reasoning question. Be sure to emphasize great—not mediocre or wimpy (they love your use of their jargon). Then, list the great reasoning questions on the board and select the best by consensus. A prize might be given to the group with the most clever reasoning question—perhaps a box containing a reward for the best out-of-the-box thinking! Offer rewards only at the beginning of your training students in thinking for themselves. After a while, success becomes its own powerful reward and tangible rewards are meaningless.

Take this activity to the next level: a competition for the best short paragraph answer to this superb reasoning question. Writing solidifies thinking and takes reasoning to a higher level. This is called *mediation of challenge*. By doing this, you are lifting your expectations above their levels of performance, taking them higher.

When the components of peer interaction, adult mediation, the use of oral language to reach consensus, and written responses are incorporated into a lesson, intellectual abilities are enhanced. The weaker students learn from the stronger and the teacher learns to ask questions that are thought-provoking. This kind of review of material adds a skylight to the roof and eases the pressure of performance on the test. Surprisingly, it often takes less time than a worksheet and is far more engaging.

In subsequent sessions, have students review a list of the questions found at the end of chapters in textbooks and then rate them as fact or reasoning. You might even have them rewrite the fact questions to turn them into reasoning questions. Have them add a dash of humor to their questions or some interesting variety in wording. Make their learning relevant and fun.

Students thrive on novelty, humor, and competition. Laughter is a great stress diffuser and therefore a great way out of the pressure cooker for all. In approaching any academic task with a sense of adventure and fun, the information to be learned will be more readily assimilated than through a tedious drill. Students will learn to generalize reasoning into other academic areas, and teachers will have gained important skills of teaching how to learn with a smile. How I wish Miss Scott had smiled at me just once in my difficult fourth-grade year!

REFLECTION

The tyranny of the urgent should not drive teaching styles or delivery of information. The pressure of deadlines, time lines, and struggling learners not able to cope with the curriculum and assessment demands can keep a teacher from truly teaching. In order to break free, be willing to change. Begin slowly by planning to remove one worksheet this week and replace it with the kind of activity described here. Get students talking to one another about what they are learning. Build their confidence and competence by entrusting them with a challenging, collaborative assignment. Then evaluate it afterward. How did we do? Let your students observe you reflecting on your questioning skills and even make recommendations for how you could improve next time. Praise good thinking. Then begin to see those comprehension skills improve. Above all, have fun with the new experiments in learning. Make it an adventure.

It has long been my belief that teachers need to take a course in drama and develop a keener sense of humor. So much happens in a classroom that is very funny, but if we are so caught up in the pressure cooker of memorization for test passing or the intensity of learning in general, we miss the joy and delight of discovery. Laughter diffuses everyone's tension, both yours and your students'. Here is a fun story to share with your students.

Our eleven-year-old grandson, Keith, was delighted to have a new baby brother. He had waited for years for his new playmate. To his surprise one-month-old baby Cole was not interested in play. Keith would come home from school and ask, "Mom, is he still just lying there?" One day his Mom overheard Keith whispering in Cole's ear, "Cole, this is your big brother, Keith. Blink twice if you can hear me!"

The need to communicate is real!

As you give permission for humor while maintaining respect for each student, you create a classroom that is affirming and pleasant. And as you encourage interactive oral language, you enable those students who do know how to learn help those who lack clear strategies for learning.

A sense of humor and a dramatic flair are important qualities that build on the propensity of learners to become more cognitively competent. We will explore these ideas more fully in the next chapter, where we take a good look at the qualities every teacher should have to be successful.

CHAPTER THREE

WHAT EVERY TEACHER NEEDS

"Don't worry about the past, you can't change it, but make every new day your masterpiece."

JOHN WOODEN

THIS CHAPTER is about you. We will be talking about self-concept, cultural literacy, love of learning, and general aptitude as a teacher. In fact, we will be traveling back to those interesting middle school–junior high years when learning went into high gear and so did peer pressure. We are all survivors of those perilous years and probably have scars or maybe even stars or bright spots that remain from them. It may help to reflect on those experiences, for as humbling as they may have been they shaped our minds and hearts as educators in interesting ways. What was your story? I will continue mine.

A GOLD COIN

It was 1956, and our family was going west. The small town of Bridgeville, Delaware, held little challenge for my father, who would spend a lifetime searching in vain for the right job. His family dutifully followed him, all four children and wife. I packed my bags happily, being ever ready for the next new experience. Our small-town eastern life was about to be traded for a western adventure in California!

The move happened to coincide with my first year of junior high school, a most unfortunate coincidence. In fact, I attended five junior high schools (grades 7, 8, and 9) in a period of three years while my father continued his frantic pursuit of a job that matched his considerable talents. And if life at school was unsettling, life at home was becoming more so. The shouting and misery on the home front escalated. It was when I was in the seventh grade that I learned that my father was an alcoholic. I wept with my mother and then decided I would be her best friend, a decision I later learned would drive a wedge between my parents.

Supporting my mother was a very difficult assignment for my adolescent mind and heart. We were moving continually into different rented properties, most of them barely adequate. I remember walking into each new school with a new lump in my throat and a growing fear that I would not make friends. And I did not have many. It was easier to try to go it alone. A certain resilience—I called it later "iron in my soul"—began to form. I remember reading *The Grapes of Wrath* and thinking, "We are a lot like the Joad family!"

School happened, and I must have learned while I attended classes, but those years are a blur. My mother told me that I grew up much faster than my peers. I learned to juggle responsibilities for my three younger brothers and became more proficient in helping to shoulder my mother's grief. Our fragile family of six lived day to day, consumed with our own needs. One day groceries were delivered to our door by an anonymous friend, and my father threw them into the front yard. Charity was totally unacceptable for him.

Then, an amazing thing happened. In the midst of being propelled from one school to another, I won a speech contest and was invited to present to the Lion's Club of Riverside, California. I had managed to learn a long poem through endless practicing and was given school- and citywide recognition. The scars of my junior high years could not blot out this bright, shining-star event. For years afterward, I would rehearse to myself "The Leak in the Dike" by Phoebe Carey. It became a significant island of competence in my ever-changing world.

I do not remember being considered particularly intelligent at this stage of my life. Rather, my goal was to survive. Amazingly, my love of learning continued to be strong, and my desire to be a teacher lay dormant, just below the surface. The junior high years produced attitudes and beliefs that shaped my character and my destiny. I learned to work hard and not complain. I became sensitized to those who were lonely and carried heavy burdens. I learned to persevere in spite of tremendous odds, and I learned that school was important. Each new experience gave me lots of practice in adjusting. Education was valued in our home; whiners were not.

My mother had earned a bachelor's degree in economics in the days when most women did not attend college. However, she was prevented from working because it was too great a challenge to my father's pride. He had no college degree and felt very overshadowed by his educated wife. His desire to be educated, however, was intense, and he grieved that he had missed his opportunity. He was determined his children would not.

I learned responsibility as the oldest child in the family. And I learned what it was like to be lonely and different and forever the new kid on the block. These, it turns out, were powerful lessons that built both the resilience and the sensitivity I would need in my future career as a teacher. I was quite a mousy teenager, younger and smaller than my peers, with bad skin and curly red hair. Not exactly a terrific combination in the sophisticated teenage world of southern California. But I now had a gold coin in my pocket: I was a speech contest winner. That could never be taken away from me.

LET'S GET PERSONAL

What is your story? Reflect on your middle school years. Were you popular or unpopular? Or were you just one of the crowd who did not stand out one way or another? For every middle school student, an *island of competence* (Brooks and Goldstein, 2003) is a safe place to stand during the turbulent preadolescent years. What was your island? The way you see your own competence and confidence today may have roots in those emerging experiences so strongly reinforced by your peers in middle school. Both positive and negative input registers long after those years have passed. For sure, emotions trump cognition.

STOPANDTHINK

Reflect about your island of competence that may have emerged in preadolescence. What about a lake of incompetence? Are these still with you today? Discuss this with a spouse or friend.

A SURVEY

What does every teacher need? Our educational system is different today than when we went to school, yet teachers' basic needs remain the same.

The following are important qualities for teachers to possess. Let's do a quick assessment. Be brutally honest with your answers. Are you:

- A lover of reading, inclined to read for pleasure as well as for information?

- Endowed with an intellectual curiosity that searches for answers through wonder and reflection?

- Connected to your culture so that cultural literacy and a broad band of knowledge can be easily transmitted to your students?

- Enthusiastic about learning and gaining new information, modeling this enthusiasm so that it is contagious?

- Competent and confident in your profession?

In this brief list, you have probably identified areas of relative strength and weakness. And, perhaps, you are reflecting on the areas needing development while celebrating your strengths. "A good teacher" is a very difficult concept to quantify, so this is by no means an exhaustive list of qualifications. It is merely a starting place. Let's examine each in more detail.

Love of Reading

Some startling statistics are coming out of our schools of education today. Many new teachers do not like to read (Moats, 2006). In fact, researchers are documenting that we are becoming an aliterate society. That is, we prefer to surf the Internet or watch the news rather than read a book or the newspaper. Declining sales of newspapers and magazines support this theory.

A love of reading is likely to surface during the middle school years. If this did not happen for you, it may have been because reading was a challenge for you, too difficult to overcome. It is far more acceptable to take the position that you do not like to read rather than admit that it is hard for you to do. We now understand the complexities of reading far better than we did twenty years ago. For example, we now know that an inability to read does *not* correlate with low intelligence. Many very intelligent people have difficulty reading. Remember our working definition of intelligence from Chapter One: "the ability to make meaningful connections."

If you scored high marks on the love of reading, congratulate yourself, your parents, and your middle school teachers, for each played a role. If you are mildly interested in reading, work on that skill. Certainly, your teaching abilities rest in some important ways on your reading proficiency and your love of good books.

We will see in later chapters that interactive language between teachers and students forms the DNA of "how to learn." If you do not read for pleasure and information, you are less able to use oral language well and have fewer vocabulary words at your disposal. If you dislike reading, you may need to consider the possibility that in your middle school years, when you had to read for content, and when the volume of information increased with each grade level, reading became a chore for you because of certain weaknesses in the reading process.

The good news, as we discussed in Chapter Two, is cognitive modifiability. The reading brain is open to change throughout a lifetime. Again, we are not talking about intelligence here. Certain cognitive systems need strengthening in order to develop reading proficiency. Reading more tends to reinforce those systems. Try reading aloud to a spouse or colleague and then stopping to discuss the material. This activity strengthens both fluency and comprehension and can be great fun. Try this with one of your favorite classics. I have just rediscovered *Gone With the Wind* after many years, and it is even more enjoyable than it was the first time I read it. I have learned some new things about that era in our country communicated more deeply than the film ever could. Relish the language and vocabulary of the classics.

Intellectual Curiosity

Would you consider yourself to be a curious person? Often, this trait develops in the home with naturally curious parents who model the wonder. To me, it seems to be an essential skill for teachers to possess, whether the trait is naturally endowed or purposefully acquired. If we ourselves do not wonder and reflect, how can we motivate a student who has no desire to learn?

Nothing stifles the development of intellectual curiosity more than a lack of interesting, curiosity-seeking role models. Another factor that stifles it is an inability to read fluently. In our highly literate society, those who cannot read (as well as those who do not read) are quickly relegated to second-class citizenship. We have put a high priority on literacy that both demands and reinforces intellectual curiosity and critical thinking.

Is there a way to develop your intellectual curiosity? Begin by making a list of all the things you are curious about. For example, take a very common subject: birds. Did you ever wonder where birds go during storms that are blowing the tree limbs everywhere? Or why we rarely see dead birds on the ground? Is there a bird graveyard somewhere? It would be great if your curiosity crossed subject areas. What about history, current events?

Share the list of your wonderings with your students. You may be surprised that they are curious about some of the same things. Some students may even be able to provide interesting answers. For the unanswered questions, go on a quest to find out. See who can be the first to bring back resolutions. In general, model curiosity in any area or in the specific subject you are studying. Prepare in advance of lessons to have an "I wonder...." question. This can be expanded to an "I wonder what would happen if...." activity. You will not only be growing your own intellectual curiosity but will be building it in your students.

STOPANDTHINK

Do you ever say to your class, "I am really *curious* about the answer to the question you just raised. I love your thinking, and the first thing I will do when I get home tonight is to look it up!"

Every teacher should be gifted with the ability to model a love of learning and a desire to find answers. In our content-driven classrooms, I fear we have lost some of the wonder of discovery. If you are naturally strong in this area, perhaps you should be conducting in-services for your colleagues.

Let's return to Aesop. I wonder if he was curious?

The Crab and the Fox

 A crab once left the seashore and went and settled in a meadow some way inland, which looked very nice and green and seemed likely to be a good place to feed in. But a hungry fox came along and spied the crab and caught him. Just as he was going to be eaten up, the crab said, "This is just what I deserve, for I had no business to leave my natural home by the sea and settle here as though I belonged to the land."

This fable promotes several "I wonder" questions:

- I wonder what crabs eat?

- I wonder if crabs are solitary creatures or if they travel in groups?

- I wonder if a crab would really prefer a meadow to the sea?

- I wonder if foxes would eat crabs?

- I wonder what lesson Aesop was teaching here? What might he have been curious about?

- I wonder where I belong? What are my true gifts and abilities?

I believe it is important for us to ask this last question regarding our profession as teachers as it relates to our particular gifts and abilities. You are a teacher because of a number of circumstances and decisions you have made over your lifetime. I completely disagree with the statement, "Anyone can teach." The art and science of teaching require certain specific skills, such as the ones we have been examining in this chapter. Most of you resonate with these abilities and continue to refine and strengthen them.

For some, there may be a growing realization that your gifts and your profession do not mesh. In this case, it is important to carefully examine your call. There is a need for honest assessment for the sake of the children we teach. If you are not comfortable reading for pleasure or have not developed an intellectual curiosity, perhaps teaching is not for you. In contrast, your commitment to improving these skills could be a transforming moment. When you overcome limitations, you open the skylight. Our minds continue to be malleable and open to change throughout the lifetime.

Ask a colleague to point out the teaching gifts he or she sees in you. Share the areas you would like to develop and explore together ways of gaining both competence and confidence.

Cultural Literacy

The concept of cultural literacy has been around since Hirsch (1988) wrote a book by that title. It is defined as a body of information that all literate members of a culture are expected to know. Only a small fraction of what we read and hear gains a secure place on our memory shelves. But the information on those "shelves" is the foundation of our public discourse. It allows us to understand our daily newspapers, our peers, and our leaders and even to share our jokes.

The concept of a body of general knowledge that all students in a particular country or culture should know may have been one of the factors behind the move toward standardization of content in our nation's schools. Cultural literacy should not be confused with specialized knowledge. It is, rather, that which keeps us American, or English, or French. To be culturally literate is to possess the basic information needed to thrive in the modern world and in a specific culture.

How can we evaluate our competence in this body of general knowledge? I was curious about my own, so I found Hirsch's *Dictionary of Cultural Literacy* (1988) and decided to browse through it. This helpful tool should be on every teacher's shelf. It will not only give you an idea of your own strengths or weaknesses in this area but will help you build your students' general knowledge of their culture. In addition, there are now graded dictionaries of cultural literacy also written by Hirsch that are most helpful.

Those with learning difficulties, incidentally, have difficulty relating to their peers in large part because they lack general cultural awareness and specific cultural knowledge. Good teachers build this knowledge base every day as they share from their personal "shelves" that which specifically defines us as a particular culture. Evaluate your own knowledge of cultural literacy. In fact, make it a goal to read an interesting biography of a famous person each year. The increase in your cultural knowledge will be a great by-product.

Love of Learning

Enthusiasm for the learning process is a given for all who teach. But as I have spent time observing teachers in schools, I have seen that this enthusiasm seems to be threatened by the pressure to cover content in a limited amount of time. Worksheets fly back and forth, two or three per lesson. Fill-in-the-blanks has all but replaced classroom discourse. What is a teacher to do? The tests must be passed and students need the facts. New information comes at them like a freight train. How can any teacher remain enthusiastic about gaining new information when a virtual stream of new information is endlessly generated?

Yet I have observed certain veterans who seem unruffled by the volume of content and have kept their enthusiasm for the learning process. They seem to have preserved their own love of learning despite the pressures that are rising to new heights. They embrace the challenges that for others may seem a deterrent in their personal and professional development. For these teachers, the challenges of the standards-based policies only deepen their desire to infuse learning with meaning and relevance. What is their secret?

Difficulties often bring out the gold in these individuals for whom teaching is more than a career. They love children and are completely invested in changing lives. They embrace the need to teach content but do it in a way that continues to make learning meaningful for students and themselves. In a word, they have found the skylights and have learned to move fluidly from the *how* to the *what* and back again. Find a colleague like that and watch him or her teach.

Students gain much from those who reflect joy in the learning process. How can you recapture the joy? We will discuss this at length in our last chapter, but let's not go there yet! In the meantime, watch a veteran. You know who they are in your school. Contagious optimism can be passed from teacher to teacher.

Competence and Confidence

Now some honest assessment in the quietness of your own space. How truly competent do you feel as a teacher? Do you think that your undergraduate and graduate studies adequately prepared you to teach? Did the courses you took provide the tools necessary for teaching? I have heard many say they were not well prepared in their schools of education to face the challenges that present themselves today. It is important to learn continually. Growing in competence means continually assessing our methods with an openness to change. Students and cultures have changed. So must we.

Realizing that we are *modifiable* is the first hurdle. With a willingness to grow, we can become more competent in our profession. Competence is a cognitive skill. We need to sharpen our skills and understanding through workshops, courses, and graduate work. Confidence, in contrast, is an affective or emotional quality. Usually, the confidence to learn and change and experiment with new ideas precedes the feeling of competence in using those skills. So the more important question is how confident are you that you can break out of an old paradigm and try something new? I hope that this book will challenge you to look toward your own personal skylight.

REFLECTION

Two more important qualities that every teacher needs should be mentioned in closing this chapter. I call them *playfulness* and a *sense of connectedness.* These may seem trivial compared to the other qualities we have covered in this chapter, but they actually enhance and undergird the others.

As I have watched teachers in action, it seems to me that those with a healthy combination of playfulness and strength foster the most engaging learning atmospheres. Humor is a vital component of a thriving learning environment. The pressures of content coverage seem to have made us more serious and intense in our delivery of information to students. Nothing diffuses stress like laughter.

Rather than putting a content slide on the overhead projector at the beginning of a lesson, try a funny cartoon or let a student tell a joke that relates to the subject. You may want to offer rewards for the funniest. If you are not blessed with a natural sense of humor, watch those who are and model their style. Be playful with your students, understand their banter, and connect to their interests. This is particularly important in middle school where the love of learning is crystallized, and adult role models who reflect playfulness become increasingly important. You know who these teachers are. Spend time with those who radiate the fun of teaching.

STOPANDTHINK

Would your students say you love learning and are happy to be a teacher? Do you have fun in your classroom? How many times a day do you laugh while teaching? Is a smile always just under the surface?

The concept of connectedness relates to both students and peers. Being able to connect meaningfully with students in a playful, lighthearted manner while communicating strength and genuine care and concern for them is an art. Connecting to your peers, fellow teachers in your school, is equally important. Research is reporting that the single greatest influence on the professional practices of teachers is the direct observation of other teachers (Reeves, 2008). I have mentioned several times in this chapter that observing a teacher who demonstrates a particular quality is a great way to learn. It also brings affirmation to a fellow professional.

Schools that develop grade-level teams provide an excellent vehicle for professional connectedness. When there are shared goals and collaborative passions, it benefits students and teachers alike.

As I reflect back on my school years, most of my teachers were unmarried and seemed very lonely. I do not think they got together professionally very often. They were stoic, set in their ways, and strong disciplinarians. There are some like that today. Education really has changed very little in fifty years. But teachers must change. Be willing to reflect on your skills and aptitudes in the qualities that we have discussed in this chapter. Examine your call. Do you possess what every teacher needs? If you do not, are you willing to go after it? Remember, change is forever possible.

In the next chapter we will turn in another direction and look beyond you, the individual teacher, to the big picture. And what a picture it is.

CHAPTER FOUR

THE BIG PICTURE

"Our curricula and our pedagogy heavily emphasize analysis over synthesis, which is the distinguishing feature of the creative impulse."
M. TUCKER, CREATING A NEW COURSE FOR SCHOOLS

IT SEEMS to be our western mentality to teach facts rather than explore ideas. We are analysts raised in a culture of analytical pedagogy. All of us have studied Bloom's taxonomy at some point in our educational careers. According to his hierarchy, synthesis is a higher-level skill than analysis. Yet we are great analysts and seem to be forever perpetuating this strength with each generation. Let's define some terms:

FIGURE 4.1.   Bloom's Taxonomy

Analysis: **Separation of a whole into its component parts, such as happens on multiple choice tests or fill-in-the-blank worksheets; also known as *deductive reasoning*.**
Synthesis: **The combining of diverse concepts into a coherent whole, such as happens in essay exams; also known as *inductive reasoning*.**

I had a glimpse of the creative impulse driven by synthesis while sitting in a classroom in Jerusalem back in 1993. I was in Israel for the first time studying under Israeli educators led by Professor Reuven Feuerstein. I remember clearly how astonished I was at the way the Israeli mind worked. It was as though there was a built-in synthesis button that took every learning situation to a new level.

The *why* and *how* questions trumped the *who*, *what*, *where,* and *when* every time. Synthesis, by way of diverse conceptions, was reached in a much more interesting and divergent manner than I had ever experienced. We Americans and Europeans who sat in class marveled at the Israelis' willingness to explore alternatives to the "obvious" answers while enjoying the ensuing debate. They smiled while they were in each other's faces, relishing the trails that opened before them. We foreigners had never been taught to think that way or with that kind of intensity.

I came to understand that part of our American cultural experience is that we value convergence rather than divergence. We seem to enjoy the product much more than the process. Reaching conclusions is what we really like, not the laborious process of weighing all the options, considering various points of view, and going down "what-if?" roads. We rush to conclusions after minimal discussion and feel quite happy when the task is done. The exploration of the richness of knowledge, which can take many different trails, is what is meant by divergent thinking. We do not seem to have the patience for such diversions. In contrast, the Israelis are masters at it. Biblical evidence indicates that Jesus was too. As was Socrates. I would like to think that we who teach can learn to capture the creative impulse within every learner through purposeful redirection from convergent to divergent thinking. That is what this chapter is about.

ANALYSIS OR SYNTHESIS?

Let's return to our reflections on our own schooling and imagine ourselves back in high school. Did we master the art of learning how to learn there? Picture yourself at a desk among a series of rows facing forward, arranged to facilitate the passing and retrieving of papers. That is how most high school classrooms are still organized. The teacher lectured on the subject, you took notes, or not. If you wanted to make a comment or ask a question, you raised your hand. Most of the talking was done by the resident expert, the teacher. Students were expected to learn the material for the inevitable test so the "what to learn" was fairly well spelled out. The "how to learn" came naturally to some who knew how to make connections to concepts they had learned earlier. These were the "intelligent" ones who did not have to study long for tests because their memories helped them connect to their internal database. But as we have said, intelligence can be taught. Did our teachers know that?

Come back in time with me again. My life story may in some ways mirror yours. And how we are educated often dictates how we teach. Consider the processes of analysis and synthesis in the big picture.

ANOTHER MOVE BACK EAST

After three frustrating years in California, my father decided to return to Bridgeville to get his bearings and help his parents with their farm and market. So we moved back into the big farmhouse together and I entered tenth grade. Because I had the "gold coin" in my pocket—that is, winning the speech contest—I felt competent, at least in one area. I remained a full year younger than my peers, yet I was years ahead of them in life experiences. And despite the emotional upheavals, I still loved school and learning. Small towns, however, are very different from big cities. You can't hide in them.

In this small town my father had the reputation of being "the brightest boy ever to come out of Bridgeville." Yet the locals felt he had wasted his life. In addition to his notorious drinking problem, his reputation of being a prankster affected my teenage years. I had some of the same teachers that he had had, and they remembered Bobby Ricards. Much of their dislike for him was taken out on me. But if I had gained anything over my short life, it was resiliency. I was always up for the next challenge. It did not bother me to sit in those straight rows passing papers back and forth. In fact, it seemed to fill a need for order within the chaos that had intensified in our home. Mom and Dad were engaged in all-out warfare in which I found myself psychologically in the middle. School was calmer, more predictable. Or perhaps I should call it more analytical?

Then, happy things began to happen. My family moved out of the farmhouse and into town and I became one of the "in crowd" as opposed to those who had to take the bus to school. Bridgeville Consolidated School, grades 1 through 12, was in a beautiful brick structure right in the middle of town. Two of the most popular girls started walking to school with me and became my friends. They thought it was wonderful that I had been to California because they had never been out of the state. They also found me very smart and funny. I found myself relaxing into this new role.

As I now reflect upon it, I realize that I had learned how to survive in varied learning environments. It was as though the tough experiences of my past brought a new convergence or synthesis to my life. I had become the product of hard work, determination, and a strong desire to learn and eventually teach. The hard times had taught me much.

Indeed, I wonder how much my teachers had actually taught me. Still, I wanted to become one, more than anything else. That desire was further intensified in the person of my high school English teacher, Mr. Reynolds.

This rather austere, quiet man had bookshelves lining the walls of his classroom containing every novel imaginable. No bulletin boards, posters, or graffiti marred the pristine atmosphere within his neat rows. This man *knew* us. When it came time for us to write a book report, a silence fell over the room. Mr. Reynolds would walk purposefully toward his shelves, select a book, and then stroll up and down the rows until he found the right candidate to plumb its depths for a report. He would then quietly deposit the book on that student's desk.

I loved the mystery of it! And he honored me with all the hardest books. I felt he knew I could do it. He never gave A's; a B in his class was the best you were going to get. I worked hard for mine and loved every minute of it. He taught me to think; he expected me to think. It was from Mr. Reynolds that I learned how to write. And writing is a marvelous extension of oral speech blended with the books you have read and the thoughts you have about them. It is the essence of synthesis. My education was taking on a new dimension.

My friends and I used to talk on the way home from school. There were no cell phones or handheld video games in those days. We continued to talk when we stopped at the soda fountain for colas and peanut butter cups. We would discuss any number of things of vital importance to our social standing, and our verbal structures were highly sophisticated in the banter of the day. The power of interactive speech was playing out in my social dialogue much more richly than in school. I do not remember having many discussions or debates on any issue inside our fine brick building. The rows prevented any face-to-face encounters. But we did have lively discussions at home around the dinner table.

My father, with all his wit and charm, was a stickler for sitting down together and having a family meal. Absences from that occasion were not excused. Talk around the dinner table was encouraged; learning was valued. Despite the tension in our home there was often healthy laughter and there were always dreams. We were expected to dream and envision great things. For this was the decade of the 1960s. Anything was possible. At the time, my brothers and I had no idea how important this oral dialogue was to our intellectual development.

"Within the constraints of our genetic legacy, our brain presents a beautiful example of open architecture. Thanks to this design, we come into the world programmed with the capacity to change what is given to us by nature, so that we can go beyond it. We are, it would seem from the start, genetically poised for breakthroughs" (Wolf, 2007).

BACK TO THE CLASSROOM

How can we teach so that students become more actively involved in their own learning? Can we move beyond stimulus-response behaviorism to a more inspired, interactive model of Socratic questioning, giving students the opportunity to think aloud and reason divergently? To do so, we will need the courage to move beyond the textbook scripts and enter a whole new world of adventure and unpredictability.

For a start, let's look at the problem of the rows. Although they may be efficient for teachers, they are not so efficient for students. Many teachers today have recognized the need to group students for more interactive discussion. The premise for changing from rows to "pods," or groups of desks together, is to facilitate the dynamic of interactive language. For the saying is true:

When a teacher talks, a student listens.
When a student talks, a student learns.

The principle was developed by Vygotsky (1994) who, in his seminal work *Thought and Language,* stated simply that oral language directs and develops thinking processes. We will explore this principle with specific examples in Chapter Six. For many teachers the quiet student is the model student. Less talking, more learning. It is time we recognize that classrooms should not be like libraries. Student engagement not only directs their own learning but presents opportunities for the less able among them to hear and adopt the thinking strategies of their more able peers. Changing the physical arrangement of the room is an easy step to take. The more difficult task is learning how to guide student engagement. Let's begin by reflecting on what we believe about those students who struggle to learn and who are found in every classroom regardless of labels such as LD, ADHD, autism, and so on or private school entrance screening.

THE POWER OF THE LIE

When special education took root and developed in our nation's schools in the 1970s tares were sown with the wheat. With the mandate that all students would be served in the public schools came a strange and erroneous philosophy. It was assumed that the kindest thing to do with these struggling learners who were now sprinkled throughout our classrooms was to adjust the curriculum downward for them. In other words, the practice of compensating for their difficulties became the modus operandi for educating these students. Adjust or modify the curriculum; do not try to change the student.

It is this philosophy that has created an interesting analysis mindset in the assessment process. Giving a student a label creates categories that are easier to manage and through which funding can flow. But it does not allow for skylights. It is time we looked again at some of these decisions through the lenses of divergent thinking. Let's move beyond analysis that comes to quick conclusions and into a new consensus born of intelligent inquiry. Our methods must change.

With all that we in western cultures have learned about the brain's modifiability, it is scandalous that we should *not* do our very best to change the intellectual abilities of struggling learners. Yet in most developed nations antiquated beliefs are still held about these children. Whether these beliefs are expressed openly or just held privately in the hearts of educators, erroneous thoughts are pervasive. "It is no use to try to teach these children, they will never be good thinkers," say the skeptics. Perhaps what we really need to do is to stop adjusting the curriculum downward and instead adjust or modify the teachers. The solutions are not as difficult as they may seem. Let's begin by moving the desks.

RETHINKING THOSE ROWS

Now that we have a more interactive classroom setting, mingling fast and slow learners in a single pod of three to four desks, the real fun begins. It is imperative that you, the teacher, enforce respect for various learning styles and competencies. Set a tone of respect for diversity both in abilities to learn and ethnic or cultural backgrounds. Tolerate no criticism. All are to be valued, and the teacher's verbal affirmation of gifts should be ongoing, cheerful, fun, and sincere.

Celebrate variety by rotating students in the learning pods throughout the year. You will be shown in subsequent chapters how to specifically model and teach the power of interactive language and divergent thinking. The premise is that those who think well can learn to speak, read, and write well. You may even inspire anew the age-old family tradition of oral storytelling, sitting around the dinner table or in the backyard or on a porch swing. But first, let's be realistic. We are in the electronic age.

REAL-LIFE CHALLENGES

Many years ago I read a book by Jane Healy called *Endangered Minds* (1990) that had a profound impact on me. She hypothesized that children who watched excessive amounts of television and played numerous video games were danger-ously altering the language areas of their brains through disuse. She wondered if the language areas of the brain might be diminished when those who overuse electronic devices restrict their verbalizing.

There seems to be some supporting evidence that brains in the digital age are becoming wired in different ways (Wolf, 2007). Should this concern us? I believe so. Just as our culture is becoming aliterate—that is, preferring not to read books—we are also limiting opportunities to talk meaningfully inside our homes due to our fast-paced lifestyle. In addition, it is reported that young people have more Internet friends than friends they interact with personally (Healy, 1999). We are becoming a dangerously nonverbal society. According to Vygotsky and Feuerstein, that limits our ability to reason, to think creatively, and to solve problems. Our brains, wired for language, are languishing.

At least in school, let's try to turn this around. If students are given guided opportunities to discuss issues, reason aloud, and challenge one another's thoughts, sharper minds will result. Let's encourage healthy debate and diver-gent thinking. Creative teachers understand that this can happen while teaching the content that is mandated for the tests. Time spent now filling out endless worksheets could be far better spent discussing the subject matter. It takes a creative teacher with some well-directed questions to get the dialogue going. Because we cannot predict where the discussion will go, many teachers shy away from this uncharted territory. Yet it is the very essence of teaching how to learn. For through discussion new thought patterns emerge; new ideas are formed and reformed. And wonderfully, students and teachers become cognitively modified. To paraphrase O. W. Holmes (1993):

> **A brain once stretched by a new idea
> never regains its original shape.**

In addition to the power of oral language there is another big issue that must be addressed. Our language facility is severely hampered by today's students' inability to write legibly. This is not a small problem; it is immense.

THE CASE FOR HANDWRITING

At some point during the debates over what subjects needed to be taught in our schools the teaching of cursive writing was relegated to the back burner. This was a sad mistake with serious consequences. Watching students write today is a painful experience. In short, they hate it. Pencil grips are a bizarre blend of tortuous finger twisting; the product of their efforts is pathetic and in many cases illegible. How can language flow from your pen or pencil when the act of writing is so uncomfortable?

The big mistake, it seems to me, is to hope the computer will solve these problems. Much real writing needs to happen in school before students begin to compose on the computer. Tragically, thinking is not flowing into written expression because the mechanics of writing have not been taught from kindergarten. Watching students try to put their ideas on paper through painful contortions confirms that these cognitive and motor systems have not been properly trained.

This is a larger than life issue because we are bound by the "what to teach." If handwriting in many states is only taught briefly in the third or fourth grade, and all students are expected to learn it quickly and do all their work in cursive during that year, it is no wonder they revert to poor printing as soon as they leave the grade. We have missed the window in the younger grades when brains and fingers are most ready for such training. If a school system decided to teach and develop correct handwriting from the early grades they might see some significant changes in written language fluency as well as higher test scores. In the wider arena it has been reported that poor handwriting costs industry and businesses $30 billion per year (Will, 2005). This, even though we are a highly technological society.

AN EXERCISE

The act of writing involves many brain mechanisms. It requires simultaneous and sequential integration of attention, memory, and higher-order cognition. It is much more complex than a simple visual-motor activity. According to Dr. Rosa Hagin (Silver and Hagin, 2002), handwriting ability affects the ability to read, spell, and comprehend. It seems to me that we have thrown the baby out with the bathwater in diminishing the role of the teaching of handwriting in schools. Let's do a couple of practical activities to help emphasize the points we have been making.

- Write your first and last name in cursive, legibly.

- Now write your signature. Does your signature look different from what you just wrote? Why?

- Write your name with your eyes closed. Is there a difference?

- Now write your name with your nondominant hand, eyes open. What makes this difficult?

- Print your name with your dominant hand.

- Now try to analyze the differences you feel between cursive and manuscript.

- If you need a little more practice with this one write a sentence in manuscript and the same sentence in cursive.

When we learn to write, a specific "motor memory" develops. You tested this interesting motor memory when you wrote your name with your eyes closed. Because the memory for your name is stored in the brain and in the muscles that produce it, you do not have to think about how to write it. Both gross and fine motor coordination are required for handwriting. The large muscles of the shoulder and arm do their job while the fingers each have a specific role to play in the production of legible handwriting. There is also what Luria (1973) calls a *kinetic memory*—that is, the automatic rhythm of the physical act of writing. Much brain activity is involved just in the mechanics of getting words on paper.

You probably were not aware when you did these activities that there was much balancing, contracting, and flexing movement involved in your written production. Your brain was simultaneously stimulating some muscle groups while inhibiting others. While your eyes were open you were self-monitoring the output that you were unable to do with your eyes closed. This feedback is usually visual in the early years and changes to kinesthetic in later years. There is an awareness of movement, location of fingers in space, internal monitoring of rhythm and rate and pencil grip. No wonder writing is hard work.

In addition to the physical act of writing there is a need for revisualization—that is, memory for letters, whole word memory, visual attention to detail and spelling. If any of these cognitive systems are weak or vulnerable, writing will suffer. I have seen real suffering in schools that do not require students to write in cursive. Let's evaluate our own experience. When you compared your cursive performance to print you may have made any of the following observations:

- I found printing easier because I was never required to write in cursive.

- Cursive is easier because it flows; it doesn't stop and start like print.

- I find I print faster but cursive is more legible when I take the time to do it.

- Because I do not remember all the cursive letters, it is easier to print.

STOPANDTHINK

"Print becomes less serviceable as more rapid written work is required in school. The need to lift the pencil after each letter makes printing too slow for work beyond the primary grades" (Silver and Hagin, 2002).

PRACTICAL APPLICATION

Could it be that teaching how to learn involves teaching students to write? If this were done well in the elementary grades it is my opinion we would not be seeing such writing casualties in the upper grades. To reiterate, is it possible that there is a connection between an inability to write fluently and an inability to think or speak fluently? If we improve one will we improve another? And what about the power to think divergently? How is that related to fluency in speech, reading, and writing? There is a great need to ask these questions. Let's address them with a fable.

The Grasshopper and the Ants

 One fine day in winter some ants were busy drying their store of corn, which had got rather damp during a long spell of rain. Presently up came a grasshopper and begged them to spare her a few grains. "For," she said, "I'm simply starving." The ants stopped work for a moment, though this was against their principles.

"May we ask," said they, "what you were doing with yourself all last summer? Why didn't you collect a store of food for the winter?" "The fact is," replied the grasshopper, "I was so busy singing that I hadn't the time."

"If you spent the summer singing," replied the ants, "you can't do better than spend the winter dancing." And they chuckled and went on with their work.

As we reflect on the meaning of this fable, it seems relevant to the hand-writing dilemma. The grasshopper (in the form of our students) was so busy singing (practicing for the required tests) that she had no time to gather corn (learn how to write legibly and build the cognitive skills for automaticity and fluency). The hardworking ants learned to both write and prepare for the tests. They were ready. The grasshopper was not, and so was ridiculed. Our students may well be spending their winters dancing.

Beyond its relevance to learning handwriting, this wonderful story can lead students into some quality thinking, both divergent and convergent. Put the fable on an overhead projector, but before showing it ask students what they know about ants and grasshoppers. This could be a purely verbal activity or it could incorporate written responses. Have students work with a partner to make two lists: one for ants and one for grasshoppers. At the top of the page list ways they are alike and at the bottom the ways they are different. Then have them compare these lists with another dyad (group of two) and have a competition to see which foursome has the most in each category. Now project and read the fable.

Here are some questions to promote strong divergent thinking:

- Was anything you said or wrote about ants and grasshoppers confirmed in the fable?

- How might the ants be drying the corn?

- Do you think dried corn would be easy for ants or grasshoppers to eat?

- Why would the ants want to dry it?

- What word would you use to describe the grasshopper?

- Which of the two insects do you admire most? Why?

  Questions leading to convergent thinking could be:

- What lesson was Aesop trying to teach? Discuss with your partner. Then share verbally with group.

- Discuss in groups of four how the lesson in this fable might be seen in a situation in life, in this classroom, or home.

- Write your own fable using this lesson: "All hard work is rewarded." Use animals rather than insects.

REFLECTION

Given the content demands of your classroom, how might you fit in an assignment like this? Perhaps it could be an early-morning, getting-things-going activity. Or it might take the place of one of those endless worksheets during the day. It could even be part of a reading or science lesson, or an end-of-the-day treat. It needs to be fun, engaging. Bring in an ant farm or a grasshopper. Think divergently! And I hope you are realizing that these fables can be adjusted upward or downward for all grade levels. Their power lies in the embedded life lessons leading to good decision making. They also teach teachers how to ask good questions.

Other benefits of this activity are big-picture benefits. They incorporate the "what to learn" but are strongly focused on the "how." They transfer to other subjects and situations. Oral language between students directs their thinking processes, refines their vocabulary and verbal expression. Your questions promote possibilities they may not have envisioned and their answers given in a group setting build understanding in the wider group.

The writing activity following such verbal dialogue is most powerful in developing strong cognitive structures because it incorporates memory, association, and the act of writing itself that builds and enhances intelligence. But students must be freed motorically to write so that their thoughts are not inhibited. Spend some time reflecting on how you might build students' abilities to write easily and legibly. Begin by considering a discussion with your administrators regarding the enhancement of writing instruction in the kindergarten classes of your school.

Are you beginning to see the possibilities for growth in yourself and in your students? Can we be freer to explore new territories within the content requirements? Can we set students free from the doldrums of memorizing endless material for the tests? That is what the next chapter is about.

CHAPTER FIVE

SETTING STUDENTS FREE

"Studies show that students retain 70 percent of what they say as opposed to 20 percent of what they hear."

F. MINIRTH, *A BRILLIANT MIND*

UNFORTUNATELY, in today's culture, many students devalue education. To be smart is no longer "cool." Those who get A's may well be ridiculed. The pursuit of knowledge and understanding is not where our young people find their significance.

Only the most engaging teachers can motivate and interest a roomful of reluctant learners who are under increasing pressure to pass the required tests. So how do we reignite the joy of learning and set students free to wonder and pursue knowledge for its own sake? To find the answers, we come back to the art of good teaching. This chapter and the next will translate the big-picture ideas into practical applications.

Teaching is truly hard, and being smart and well educated does not make one good at it. Discipline, struggling learners, difficult home situations, and the constant pressure to have students perform well on high-stakes tests sends many well-meaning teachers into other professions. But what if these seeming constraints became opportunities?

RATCHETING UP, NOT DUMBING DOWN

Let's begin our journey into freeing students to learn by exploring our first principle:

> **Raise expectations above students' current levels of functioning.**

Now that we understand that intelligence is the continuing changing state of an individual best demonstrated by his or her ability to make connections, we know our students are capable of more than they are currently achieving. Yes, all of them are—and as I mentioned earlier, so are we. It may be helpful to reexamine this idea through a brief review of propensity and potential. Remember that potential implies a lid or ceiling, as when we say, "This child is working within his learning potential." Propensity, in contrast, is the limitless upward trajectory that assumes continuous improvement and possibility for change.

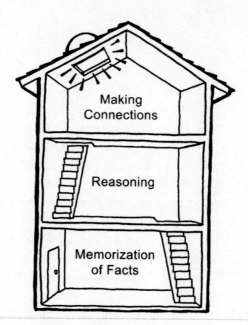

FIGURE 5.1.   The Three-Story Intellect

Another way to view intellectual propensity is the concept of the three-story intellect. This concept was first conceived by Oliver Wendell Holmes. This great American writer won praise throughout the late 1800s for his essays and poems. He was known for his keen mind and witty literary style. His enthusiasm for teaching and learning kept his Harvard medical students openly engaged and actively interested, even to the last period of the day. Holmes explored the workings of the mind in the magazine he helped launch, the *Atlantic Monthly*, still in circulation today. Some of his rambling thoughts around the breakfast table are instructive:

I don't want to have the territory of a man's mind fenced in. I don't want to shut out the mystery of the stars with the awful hollow that holds them. We have done with those temples that were open above to the heavens, but we can have attics and skylights to them. Minds with skylights—yes, stop, let's see if we can get something out of that.

One-story intellects, two-story intellects, three-story intellects with skylights. All fact collectors, who have no aim beyond their facts, are one-story men. Two-story men compare, reason, generalize, using the labors of the fact collectors as well as their own. Three-story men idealize, imagine, predict. Their best illumination comes from above, through the skylight. There are minds with large ground floors that can store an infinite amount of knowledge. Some librarians, for instance, who know enough of books to help other people without being able to make much other use of their knowledge, have intellects of this class.

Your great working lawyer has two spacious stories; his mind is clear because his mental floors are large and he has room to arrange his thoughts so he can get at them; facts below, principles above and all in ordered series. Poets are often narrow below, incapable of clear statement and with small power of consecutive reasoning, but full of light, if sometimes rather bare of furniture in the attics.

Holmes's *The Poet at the Breakfast Table* was written in 1882. His ideas present a wonderful model that begs the question he did not answer: "What is the skylight?" For this is as far as he went with his conceptualization of three-story intellects. So let's take some liberties to deepen and refine his desire not to have the territory of a man's mind fenced in.

The First Floor

In the view we will take on thinking and learning, the first floor is the place where memorization of facts occurs. Those with one-story intellects rely primarily on memorization for their learning. These are the students who spend much time in rehearsal of facts in order to succeed in school. It does not seem to matter to them that they do not understand the material. Many learners are content to stay right here, on the ground level.

The Second Floor

Those with second-story intellects have taken a more comprehensive view. They understand that reasoning is a necessary component in the learning process. They have learned over time that memory alone will not serve them. They need to ask the "why" questions. Facts must be learned, so they combine fact learning with understanding and begin making meaning of the information taught. In a sense they have the use of both floors and often use them very well, like the lawyer in Holmes's view. Some educated people are content to stay at the second-story level, not even realizing that another may exist.

The Third Floor

Those who move on to the third story often need to be taken there by a teacher who understands the power of intellectual transformation that can happen for all students, not just the seemingly intelligent ones. It has much to do with the teacher's skills of mediation. The rarified air at this level is the brilliance of making connections beyond simply understanding the facts. It involves connecting meaningfully with past experiences, comparing past, present, and future events, recognizing principles, and making application to life issues. Third-story intellects press through the hard places to find answers. They have been trained to see patterns of similarities and differences and are able to recognize cause and effect. They can explore alternatives without having to rush to conclusions. Many who arrive here never want to leave, until they look up and notice the skylight.

Oliver Wendell Holmes is known for another saying:

> **Every now and then a man's mind is stretched by a new idea or sensation and never shrinks back to its former dimensions.**

Putting in the Skylight

This was, I believe, what Mr. Holmes meant by putting the skylight in the roof. There is no fourth-story intellect. Those who learn how to learn transcend the knowledge and insights of their teachers. They learn that there are no limits to discovery, creativity, and scholarly pursuit.

Students of all ages are fascinated by their own brains. Having a colorful, informative poster of the brain on the wall or a model of the three-story intellect will keep the message current: "Together, we are building better brains!" Students who have opted out of learning for a variety of reasons may receive fresh insight when they realize that learning and changing is what the brain really wants to do. Connecting to what motivates individuals to think and learn is the art of good teaching. And getting them to talk about these things is truly teaching at its best. This leads us to our second important principle:

> **Oral language develops good thinkers and moves students along the upward trajectory toward the skylight.**

The task of building a vibrant, literate community belongs to you, the teacher. Students need to know how important it is for them to speak well in order to develop their own thinking processes. You can set the tone by valuing intellectual curiosity, inspiring wonder, and freeing students to discover their propensity. Many are bound in the "I can't" mentality. Or they are stuck in the boredom trap. They seem to have lost their natural, God-given curiosity.

Albert Einstein said, "I have no special talent. I am only passionately curious."

Passion is contagious. Share yours. Get them to talk about what fires them up. Affirm their gifts within the dynamic, literate community you are building. In their "pods," have them ask each other questions on what they are passionate about. How do they spend their free time? What are they interested in?

This "interest polling," best achieved at the beginning of the school year, could yield "resident experts" on specific subjects who could be referenced regularly. As lessons are approached, the expert could be the first to share knowledge on that topic. Oral language has the power to produce exciting, vibrant classrooms. Remember, the most effective instruction lets students talk and guides the development of clear, logical thinking. As students hear the passions of others they are often inspired to turn off the television and get involved in a meaningful hobby or activity that will take their minds into their own third stories with skylights!

Realistically, in our age of information overload it is difficult to inspire wonder and a desire to learn. Students can find answers at the click of a mouse. Some, because of the data glut, have forgotten what it felt like to be curious about anything. You, the teacher and master mediator, must regularly model your love of learning and the wonder it inspires in you. "Guess what I learned last night?" would be a good beginning to any day.

Plan to start a particular lesson with an "I wonder" thought. For example, "I wonder if global warming is actually happening. It seems there is research from the scientific communities that supports both positions. It certainly seems the media has confirmed it. Would it not be wise to consider that it is open to debate and to explore this important topic beyond what the newspapers are saying?" Initiate discussion by having students express their thoughts and perhaps divide into teams to research their position. Give them assignments to collect facts that support their positions. Healthy debate is one of the most productive ways to build critical thinking skills. These are profitable times of learning and information gathering that have nothing to do with passing a test but everything to do with building third-story intellects that are willing to listen to another person's point of view.

An Interesting Lesson

Here is an example. I was recently in India with a group of students studying economics. Their teacher presented the concept of global warming and seemed to conclude that it was irrefutable. After the lesson I asked where she had collected her facts and she said, "American newspapers." I politely suggested that many scientists have differing opinions about global warming and that newspapers are not always our best source of information.

In India's race to become a dominant player in the global economy it is important that the students of that land have opportunities to think clearly about issues and engage in healthy debate well beyond what they read in the newspapers alone. This rigorous debate about issues must be encouraged in our schools, and students must be trained to do it. I fear our students have begun to think there is only one right answer: what goes on the test. This is first-story intellectual reasoning—memorization of facts. We must take students higher. Let's explore some ways to do that.

PRACTICAL APPLICATIONS

As you approach your history lesson for the day you might recall the specific expertise of your students and say, "John, I know you have a special interest in sailing. Tell us one fact about a sailboat that the rest of us may not know. Sally, ask John a reasoning question as opposed to a factual question about a sailboat. Remember, reasoning questions begin with how or why. Juan, put sailboat into a category. Do you agree, Eve?" (Allow for differences of opinion here. There are several possibilities.) "What do you think sailboats have to do with history? Did you ever wonder who built the first sailboats? How could we find out?" This discussion could lead into some interesting discoveries and is much more engaging than a simple delivery of the facts.

Your goal should be to allow student dialogue as often as possible, either in small groups (discuss in your pods who you think may have built it and for what reason) or in the large group with you facilitating the dialogue. Bring out any personal experiences with sailboats by saying, "Susan, have you ever been on a sailboat?" And then, "Let me briefly tell you my experience." This leads us to our third important principle:

Always begin a new topic by connecting students to prior experience and knowledge.

A great way to engage learners is to lead them to reflect on what they already know. Teachers must become facilitators of connections—the domain of the third-story intellect. We want to expand students' frames of reference by taking them from the known to the unknown. The art of our questioning should foster in our students a predisposition toward such cognitive expansion. Remember, the desire to understand is inherent in the human brain. We are wired for it. For those students who seem to have become disconnected, it is our belief in their propensity and our enthusiasm for the learning process that will connect them again. It is my strong conviction that a well-directed discussion of the topic you are studying trumps a worksheet every time. But teachers must have confidence in their ability to direct such a discussion. First, you must be convinced that oral language builds thinking processes, that yours must draw forth theirs.

Let's connect to another fable.

The Traveler and His Dog

 A traveler was about to start on a journey and said to his dog who was stretching himself by the door, "Come, what are you yawning for? Hurry up and get ready. I want you to go with me." But the dog merely wagged his tail and said quietly, "I'm ready, master. It is you I am waiting for."

Can you connect with Aesop's lesson in this story? There are two perspectives here, the master's and the dog's. As we try to relate the fable to our experiences it could be said that the traveler is the teacher, ready to go on not just a short walk but a journey—through another school year, or even through a lesson, for example. The dog, who could be kindly represented as a student, desires very much to go and indicates such by wagging his tail. The receptivity of the dog is not immediately noticed by the master, who seems a bit disconnected and impatient when he sees the yawning and appears not to hear the dog's musings: "Ready when you are."

How many of our students are patiently, or impatiently, waiting for us to lead them on the amazing journey of learning? They yawn or misbehave often because we do not have the correct tools to lead them out the door. Sadly, yawning is a signal that teachers often miss. The boredom in our classrooms is not always the students' fault. They are more ready to learn than we can imagine. Let's take them there.

MEANINGFUL CONNECTIONS

We must be ready to lead students into a love of learning. Do we really know them? Have we made an attempt to connect with each student relationally? I recently walked down the hall with a middle school principal who was making his morning rounds and he greeted each student he met by name, often inquiring about a specific person in that family. I learned there were fourteen hundred students in the school. That is relationship building on a grand scale. Interestingly, the discipline in this school was exemplary, the learning environments rich and productive. Teachers took the lead from the caring principal and emulated that personal touch in their classrooms.

This, I would offer, is the first step to setting students free. Know them, their likes and dislikes, their passions and frustrations. Enter into healthy, fun banter. Praise their successes openly and warmly. And always take them higher. Believing in their innate propensity will cause you to ratchet up the challenge level. And because they know you believe in them, they will amazingly rise to your expectations. Dumbing down the curriculum or your own expectations diminishes and demotivates a learner.

I once said to a struggling learner, "Eric, I see greatness in you." He lifted his head and with wonder in his eyes replied, "You do?" When I responded in the affirmative he said enthusiastically, "You mean great like Walt Disney?" From that day forward Eric had a new perspective on himself and his future. Can you imagine the pure joy of setting your reluctant learners free? Sometimes all it takes is a well-timed word.

SO WHAT ABOUT YOU . . . AND ME?

My personal journey to intellectual freedom took a giant leap when I graduated fourth in my high school class of thirty-seven (not too impressive, I agree!) and entered the University of Delaware as a freshman elementary education major, confirming my childhood dream to become a teacher. I was barely seventeen years old. True to form my parents chose this time to move back to California, so I was left all alone on the East Coast. The freedom was not exactly exhilarating. Our family unit was becoming more fragile with every year, but for the first time in my life I did not have to endure the constant battles. I was truly on my own. Remarkably, as I began to swim in a bigger pond, I learned that others had home situations that were much worse than mine. I relaxed a bit and began to find that I could make people laugh. College was more fun than I dreamed it could be.

I was so excited about becoming a teacher that I turned all my energies into my studies. You could say I was a disciplined learner but not a particularly gifted one. My European history class with five hundred students, as well as a thick, jammed-with-details textbook, boggled my mind. I received a D– in that class. In fact, in my first semester I was placed on academic probation. Eighteen credit hours was death to this freshman who had not really learned how to learn. I could memorize, but there was no way I could get around that history textbook or others like it. I remember thinking how intelligent my roommate, Sally, was. She took the same courses I did and got A's. She told me she was taught how to study in high school. Because she went to a large, urban school, such study skills classes were offered. In my tiny school I could not even take a typing course—because I was not on the secretarial track—let alone a study skills class. Limited options often create limited learners.

So when faced with a history test, Sally knew how to organize the massive amount of information and synthesize it. She had learned to make connections and to ask herself questions when she read. I had never heard of such things. Mr. Reynolds had given me a love of literature and encouraged my ability to write, but this was a different category of thinking and learning involving information gathering.

The *what to learn* became the barrier. It really was not a matter of intellectual capacity or laziness or lack of interest. I needed someone to teach me the system, the *how to learn.* So Sally did. We began to study together, talking about what we learned and what was important to remember. She helped me focus on the big ideas, and because I could memorize well I would develop subpoints under each. I do not think Sally realizes today how she helped shape my intellectual development.

What about you? Reflect on your college years and the way you processed large amounts of information. Were you like Sally, well-equipped to handle studying for a test or able to read a rather uninteresting text to extract meaning? Or were you more like me, drowning in a lake of details?

In order to connect meaningfully with your students you need to remember both your struggles and your successes. Let them know what you found difficult, but then also let them know how you persevered and mastered it. There comes a certain point when pure memorization will not do it for you. I am glad I hit my wall early in my academic career. I realized that there were other levels to my intellect, although I did not think of it in those terms. I knew I wanted to go there. The *how to learn* became a consuming passion. For if I was going to become a teacher it was very important for me to courageously face my difficulties and work through them. This, incidentally, is the next step toward student freedom.

Jamie Evans in his book *An Uncommon Gift* (1983) reflects on his learning disability as a special motivator. He learned a valuable lesson in sixth grade through an embarrassing incident when a girl he liked saw his spelling errors and laughed. He determined then and there that although his learning disability was not his fault it was his responsibility. He recognized that it was up to him, not his teachers or his parents, to work hard to overcome it. His story is inspiring. Jamie began a quest that paid big dividends. He is now a well-loved Presbyterian minister with a strong work ethic and a vibrant congregation.

Many of our young people, particularly those who find learning difficult, contract what is known as *learned helplessness*. They catch this malady from their parents and teachers who make sure they are attending to every need the student has. Adults and students alike can become bound within the prison of low expectations. This cycle can be broken, however, by becoming aware of enabling tendencies and having a sincere talk with students to plan new directions. Encouraging students to take responsibility for their learning lets them understand that you are their biggest fan but you cannot hit the ball for them. Your sincere belief in the propensity of your students will be communicated through your eyes and in your voice.

In the end, a student's decision to step up to the plate and hit a home run is an internal one brought about by his or her own realization that intelligence is malleable. As teacher you have the great privilege of introducing students to the idea of three-story intellects with skylights that are waiting for them to reach. Setting students free to learn sometimes involves your purposeful release of them.

REALISTIC DREAMS

I am concerned about current thinking that wants to sort students in elementary and middle school according to their probable destinies. While I agree with the concept of vocational education and the idea that not everyone should go to college, I do not believe we should ever suppose that that languishing sixth-grader needs to forget about AP classes.

Everyone can be taught to think well, and all professions need good thinkers. My hairdresser is one of the most widely read people I know, and he loves to talk about his knowledge. Surely, the purpose of schooling in a democracy is to create an informed citizenry who can problem-solve, reason, and reflect on the issues and challenges facing our world today. I am concerned that we are in danger of keeping students on the first story of intellectual capacity in our rush to prove they can pass the required tests. Those students are not free.

REFLECTION

Some teachers dream of dispensing information to silent students who sit in rapt reflection. There is something quite noble about this idea—exuding a knowledge for which students thirst and would stop reading their own books if only they could listen and learn from you. Most teachers only fantasize over such a scene.

In reality, the process of learning is rather messy. It requires attention, focus, discipline, and hard work. Many opt out; the rewards seem too few. After all, there are those in our society who are highly successful with only a high school education. What is the big deal about becoming a better thinker or going to college? A certain cynicism has infected our youth. Perhaps they have learned it from their parents. Can we recapture the wonder of learning for its own sake? The joy of it? It seems that many students today are not benefiting from a balance of intellect and imagination, essential ingredients in an informed and vibrant society. The Chinese philosopher Confucius said in 500 BC:

> **"This student does not help me.**
> **He completely agrees with me."**

I wonder how many teachers today would applaud Confucius's perspective. Many think that agreeing with the teacher is what students are supposed to do. But Confucius captured a schooling dilemma that remains current today. How do we develop creative, knowledgeable students who know how to ask questions themselves while maintaining respect for those with differing ideas? Students who have been encouraged to appreciate the lessons of the past are often capable of thinking for themselves about the future. In fact, they begin to delight in overcoming the barriers of generally accepted solutions in order to solve novel problems. What really distinguishes effective learners is the ability to seek and find knowledge independently, transcending the limits of their own knowledge and that of their teachers. In essence, it is the ability to find the skylight.

In order to lead students to this kind of academic freedom we must find a special way to:

- Introduce the subject matter.

- Train students to interact with adults without imitating their knowledge.

- Train students to interact with peers in a way that distributes points of view.

More about these in the next chapter.

Meanwhile, here is one final word on setting students free. As teachers we must be willing to become learners with them. We must encourage divergent thinking and rigorous, informed debate. An atmosphere of trust must be developed in the classroom so that students and teacher can disagree respectfully. We must cultivate a love of scholarship and inquiry, accepting and acknowledging differing views and opinions.

Releasing power over students' minds is difficult for teachers. The expectation is that we must fill up those empty vessels. Yet filling them with one-story intellectual capacities—that is, merely factual knowledge—does not allow them to take full advantage of their ability to teach you and their peers. Each of the challenges mentioned here will be addressed in the following chapters. The power of interactive oral language is what our next chapter is all about.

CHAPTER SIX

THE POWER OF ORAL LANGUAGE

"The way of words, of knowing and loving words, is a way to the essence of things, and to the essence of knowing."

JOHN DUNNE

FROM THE insights of Piaget, who observed and recorded student dialogue, to the understandings of Vygotsky and Feuerstein, who elaborated and refined his theories, it has become clear that students' oral language helps direct their thinking processes. The fewer opportunities students have to verbalize and refine their thoughts, the less they can develop clear thought patterns allowing them to become independent, lifelong learners. Verbalized thoughts eventually go underground and become useful inner language, but only after they are given good scrutiny by a mediator who is adept at questioning and probing for meaning. This happens, in part, through the art of Socratic questioning.

THE SOCRATIC METHOD

Socrates lived in the fifth century BC. He was an orator who understood the power of dialogue in shaping intellectual capacity. He taught students to question the words and concepts conveyed through spoken language in order to probe the beliefs that lay behind them. Interestingly, Socrates was such a believer in the power of oral speech that he himself wrote nothing (Wolf, 2007). He had a great fear that writing and the reading of books could short-circuit the work of active, critical understanding. The transition from an oral culture to a literate one concerned him greatly. He believed the uncontrolled spread of written language in place of oral language posed serious risks to society for these reasons:

- Oral and written words play very different roles in an individual's intellectual development.

- Written language places a much less stringent requirement on memory than oral language.

- Oral dialogue plays an important role in the development of morality and virtue in a society.

Socrates was unquestionably an advocate of the power of oral language. We must try to recapture some of his ideas and implement some of his methods in order to develop learners who are able to think for themselves while maintaining morality and virtue. Lev Vygotsky, in his classic work *Thought and Language* (1994), described the important relationships between thinking and speaking and teacher and learner. Reuven Feuerstein (2007) contributes the theories of cognitive modifiability and mediation of the learner. In the hands of a skilled teacher intellectual abilities take on new life.

In this chapter we will examine a literature lesson that illustrates how such questioning can probe and develop student thinking. We will also examine what Vygotsky calls the *zone of proximal development* (ZPD)—that is, an assistive social space through which students learn, with the teacher and other students, how to make meaning from the subject being studied.

THE RESEARCH

First, let's look at some history regarding classroom talk. For the past century the primary student "talk" in classrooms has been recitation. Rote reciting of facts belongs on the bottom level of the three-story intellect. This outmoded method, still used regularly in many underdeveloped countries, has been found to inhibit student thinking. In contrast, researchers have found that students' exploratory talk with peers rather than rote recitation helped make knowledge their own (Narrol and Giblon, 2001). Interestingly, this is exactly what I found many years ago as a college freshman when studying and discussing European history with my roommate Sally. Talking with others does help clarify one's thinking. You have probably found that too.

STOPANDTHINK

When was the last time you were able to come to a reasonable conclusion about a particular problem after discussing it with someone?

Several studies have affirmed the potential of students to make meaning of their lessons independently, without benefit of group recitation or even relying on the facilitation of the teacher. However, there is a limit to what students, particularly in the elementary grades (and I would argue even in the upper grades), can learn without good adult mediation. It is through the effective use of the zone of proximal development that teachers can begin to facilitate the development of students' habits of minds. This requires a teacher who can carefully frame and focus student dialogue. We will discuss specific habits of mind later in this chapter.

The rather abstract concept of the zone of proximal development is defined by Vygotsky (1994) as the distance between what a child can do alone and what he or she can do during problem solving under adult guidance. With adult mediation, higher-level cognitive functions that have not yet matured can be developed effectively through collaborative, open-forum problem solving. Admittedly, this kind of open discussion requires a specific set of skills that can be learned by both teachers and students. Critical thinking and problem solving, both necessary in today's world, require that we who teach embrace new models of instructional delivery.

The traditional elementary school of the past century was designed to prepare students for the factory or the field. Specifically, its emphasis was on motivation for conscientious labor, self-discipline, and building a set of skills for following instructions. Preparing students to think creatively, to take intellectual initiative and to challenge or modify existing models, was not the intent at the turn of the twentieth century. Yet we operate still under many of the same outdated assumptions. Consider the teaching of literature. Many teachers expect the students to follow their interpretations of literature and cut students off from their own responses.

It is time for a new paradigm: building intellectual capacity. Happily, as we have discovered, our intelligence is malleable, open to change throughout a lifetime.

Let's learn some new skills. We will take a literature sample from the book *Character Is Destiny: Inspiring Stories Every Young Person Should Know and Every Adult Should Remember,* by John McCain (2006).

This anthology of heroes who exhibit exemplary character contains historical items of interest and character studies to facilitate dialogue. McCain tells these moving stories of triumph against the odds, exemplifying the best in the human spirit. In this excerpt we will look at Winston Churchill, the well-known British statesman, and the character qualities of courage and determination.

He had returned again to Harrow, his old school, a place that had evoked memories of long-ago loneliness and disappointment. On October 29, 1941, the day he rose to speak to Harrow's students, Winston Churchill had been Britain's prime minister for just seventeen months. Harrow had expected a stirring speech. It was a short address. He removed his top hat and set it on the podium, gathered his thoughts for a moment while brushing a tear from his eye. Then he uttered the words that would become a legend, "Never give in. Never give in. Never, never, never, never—in nothing great or small, large or petty—never give in, except to convictions of honor and good sense."

He was approaching his sixty-seventh birthday. He had lived a life of extraordinary accomplishments and humiliating defeats long before he became prime minister. He had suffered a lonely and oppressive childhood. He was small, sickly, and accident-prone. He had been an unhappy and unsuccessful student. His parents were busy and famous people who cared little for his suffering. He was sent away to a boarding school at the age of eight where he was bullied terribly by the older boys. Both his mother and father blamed him for the beatings he received there. He was closer to a nanny than to his own parents, as was common in the British aristocracy of the day.

His father died never knowing [his son] would one day become prime minister. [Churchill] never gained his . . . father's approval, which was a cause of great sadness in his life. While serving as a cavalry officer he fought bravely, was captured by guerrillas, then managed a spectacular escape over hundreds of miles of hostile country, rejoined the army and became a war hero. He married Clementine, who would be the only truly close friend of his adult life. Some years afterward he lost his three-year-old daughter, Marigold, to an illness. Her death nearly destroyed him.

World War One had destroyed an entire British generation and few Britons wanted to consider the possibility of another war with Germany. So the nation and its politicians looked the other way as Hitler took power; all but Churchill who saw and spoke the danger when no one would listen. He was exposed to much public ridicule and contempt as he continued to declare there was "a gathering storm." His insight was eventually rewarded. He led England into World War Two to fight against the evil that Hitler was perpetrating in Germany. Today Churchill is remembered for his extraordinary courage and determination.

Winston Churchill, the abandoned child, the failed student, the war hero, the controversial statesmen, the scorned, reviled, and forgotten politician who stood alone against an enemy no one wanted to fight, whose life accomplishments were greater than a hundred men could produce became the king's first minister on May 10, 1940. He let no defeat, no danger, no impossibly overwhelming odds destroy his courage or his will. He would not give in. Never, never, never, never. And due in great part to the courage he inspired in others, neither would his country.

When my family returned from England in 1952, Winston Churchill was a hero. I remember bringing home a statue of the man with a removable cigar; the statue had a place of honor on our bookshelf for many years and provided an opportunity for my father to tell us stories about heroes and what they were. Our students today need heroes and heroines. They need to understand about character and determination and what it means to have a destiny. And they need to extract meaning from text with the assistance of an expert mediator, not a worksheet. They need to talk about what they are reading. Let's walk through an adventure in exploring the ZPD.

PRACTICAL APPLICATIONS

Before reading the preceding passage, have students in their "pods" discuss what they know about England. Every classroom should have both a globe and a world map. Have them locate England and describe its geographical relationship to the United States. Discuss how you would get there from here and how long it might take. Build a sense of intellectual curiosity through the question, "How many of you have ancestors from England? If you don't know, see if you can find out from your parents or grandparents." In all of these questions, draw from your students clear, concise, expressive language. For example:

TEACHER: John, can you find England on the map?

STUDENT: I see England. It is right there (pointing).

TEACHER: Can you tell me its location specifically in relation to the U.S.?

STUDENT: It is across the ocean.

TEACHER: Be specific. Tell me the compass direction, the name of the ocean, and the approximate distance from the United States. (This helps the student frame and focus a response.)

STUDENT: England is approximately 3,000 miles east of the United States across the Atlantic Ocean. (After working through sentence structure and correct use of language. This could take a couple tries with teacher mediation.)

TEACHER: Jane, do you agree?

STUDENT: I think it is closer to 4,000 miles.

TEACHER: How could we find out?

STUDENT: I could search online the distance from a point in the U.S. to a point in England.

By requiring specific and precise oral language you have helped build cognitive structures. Teachers often accept the first answer a student produces without probing and helping to construct clear responses. Drawing out and helping to form student responses is precisely what is meant by mediation. Adult mediation of student responses creates an assisted learning space, the ZPD, that enables the student to think more clearly about the subject—in this case, geography.

Explore the names of famous people who came from England. Your students may know more than you think. Have each group generate as many names as they can think of in one minute. Reward the longest list. If Winston Churchill is not mentioned, begin to write his name on the board one letter at a time and see who can guess it first. This famous statesman should be on students' cultural literacy shelves at least by middle school. Prompt this "what-they-already-know" phase by saying, "This man was in for a big surprise and he also had a great secret. What he was like as a young boy was nothing like what he would become. Give some ideas on what you think happened."

Now show students the book and briefly discuss the author. This man, John McCain, is a public figure in the United States today. You may want to open some political dialogue. Remember, debate is healthy and teaches children how to understand various points of view, always respectfully.

Oral reading by the teacher to the class is a powerful tool to develop both listening and visualizing skills. Also, students will hear your fluency with spoken words and begin to model that in their own reading. Be sure to use expression, drama, and tone to tell the story. Be engaging. Just before reading the first paragraph ask students to try to picture the scene.

After reading the first paragraph stop and ask the following questions:

- How did Winston Churchill feel about his old school?

- What kind of school was it?

- What may have happened to him there that caused his sadness?

- How do you think the author feels about Churchill?

- What picture came to your mind as you were listening?

- Who can read the statements Mr. Churchill made to his former school using the tone he may have used?

Then say, "Sally, tell us what you think a prime minister is." Do not be tempted to tell or teach at this point; let students explore their thoughts and you be a learner with them. Facilitate the discussion by saying, "Juan, do you agree?" after Sally has expressed her thoughts. Then, after a few have given ideas, ask, "Jason, what does *prime* mean?" Give some time for discussion before asking for a definition of minister.

This kind of open-ended inquiry is at the heart of Socratic questioning. Depending on the answers your students offer you may be led to briefly draw from students what differences they think there are between the structures of government in the U.S. and Great Britain or the boarding school versus public school comparisons. Limit your oral interactions to five to ten minutes. Resist the temptation to tell them everything you know. Allow them the joy of discovery. Leave them wanting more.

Continue reading the next paragraph, then ask, "Sam, can you summarize the paragraph?" After Sam has given his response, affirm him and then say, "Now take Sam's summary and see if you can improve on it in your small groups. I will read the paragraph aloud again." Have a spokesperson from each group give the oral summary. Allow only five minutes. As responses are read, help clarify oral language (students will learn to expect this) and praise good thinking. It is often appropriate to say, "Could someone else say it a little more clearly and more to the point?"

Finish reading the excerpt and then ask, "What was Winston Churchill's great secret? What was the surprise? How can we apply those secrets and surprises to our lives today?" Notice there are no specific right or wrong answers. The open discussion helps students make meaning from the literature without having to read a word of it. Those who struggle with reading are on an even par with those who do not. Listening skills are developed and vocabulary expanded. And these answers produce no poor worksheet grades.

Students should always be exposed to oral language that is above their reading level. You can come back to various words in the passage to get clear definitions or to extract meaning. As a culminating activity give a copy of the passage to each group. Now read it again with great expression and drama while they follow along.

If you have an excellent reader who can model fluency and expression, have that student read. Now take one paragraph and have the whole class read it together. This becomes recitation with meaning because it follows oral discussion and takes your students into the second-story intellect—reasoning and understanding. Research shows us that repeated oral reading builds fluency necessary for automaticity as well as comprehension. Building processing speed reinforces weak and vulnerable cognitive systems. This is *how to learn* at its best.

A New Kind of Learner

The learning activity just discussed takes students beyond traditional education into an experience of reflective intelligence. The ideal student in this new way of thinking is not the one who gives correct answers and repeats what the teacher has said but rather the one who asks questions and accepts and expects a variety of points of view. What really distinguishes this authentic learner is not profound and extensive knowledge or even a brilliant display of what one has learned. Instead it is the ability and incentive to gain knowledge independently. This, as we have said, depends on the teacher's expertise in several areas:

- *Introducing the subject matter:* Providing students with the opportunity to relate to that which they already know gives them a point of reference and develops important cognitive connections. Thinking about what they already know about England primes the mind for comparisons. Some students may have visited there and can share actual experiences that enrich the lesson. Finding England on the map provides an anchor to the story. Many students are clueless about geography. Help them build these mental maps.

- *Training students in a special way of interacting with an adult:* Students should not anticipate quick solutions or answers from their teacher. Instead, there should be an expectation that their teacher will guide them to find answers for themselves. The teacher's assistance will provide opportunity for everyone to transcend their own thinking. This, I have found, is one of the most difficult transitions for teachers to make. We like to tell what we know rather than allow students the joy of discovering for themselves. Train yourself to say, "I am not sure. Sally, what do you think?" Allow students the freedom to challenge your thoughts, always respectfully. Become a learner with them. Their discussions about Winston Churchill's experiences in boarding school may yield ideas you never thought of. Always praise good thinking.

- *Promoting peer interaction:* Ensuring that students are positioned in the classroom for group discussions leads to the distribution of various points of view. As we have discussed, groups or pods should include students of varying intellectual strength and should change periodically over the year. Once you have affirmed the expectation that there are collaborative assignments and that each has a part to play, you will be surprised at the willingness of students to contribute. Competition is always fun. Which group can come up with the longest list of people from England or things that remind you all of England? They will learn to moderate their voices so as not to give away their lists.

By now I am sure you are wondering how all of this will really work in light of the impossible demands on your time in covering the subject matter. I hope you have begun to see some new ways to bring change that may even be exciting and worth trying. Let's go back in time again to your very first teaching experience. Here's mine.

ORAL OBSTACLES

Having somewhat mastered the textbooks at the college level, my passion to teach intensified. But there continued to be barriers. In my senior year I found I was an appalling orator. My public speaking class at the University of Delaware produced such panic in me that I actually prayed I would be hit by a truck before reaching the class in which I was to deliver my first speech. Fortunately, God, as before, saw fit not to respond.

As I stood before my peers my knees knocked audibly and if that were not bad enough, my voice trembled with such intensity that those listening shook their heads to try to understand what I was saying. I have learned since that the fear of public speaking is the number-one phobia reported in polls. I was right there. Not a great omen for one who wanted to be an orator for life. And how could I possibly have won that speech contest? Could I really do this thing . . . teach? Then, a new path opened.

I met my knight in shining armor who rode gallantly into my life to rescue me from my troubled childhood. We were married in Newport, Rhode Island, on the day he was commissioned as a naval officer. Immediately we began to get "orders." First stop, Norfolk, Virginia, where I would have my first teaching assignment. It was pure bliss. I had one of those perfect classrooms with a well-behaved group who responded to me with "Yes, ma'am" or "No, ma'am." It was music to my Yankee ears.

We were in a brand-new school where there were yet no chalkboards hung and supplies were late in arriving. But I found I could stand in front of those precious faces and speak without trembling. And they learned, amazingly. Because it was all new and fresh, like my marriage, little frustrations were ignored and the wonder of finally becoming a teacher became a new gold coin in my pocket to join the speech contest honor. I could scarcely contain the joy.

Can you remember similar feelings from your first teaching experience? If not your first year, try to remember your best year and reflect on why it was so good. What can you recapture from those years? I suspect it was an attitude of expectancy that motivated you to believe great things were going to happen for the children in your class. Sadly, we become more cynical over the years and students tend to sense it. We lose the wonder. There is a way to get it back. It involves cultivating new habits of the heart and mind.

Habits of Mind

The first important habit of mind that needs to be established is the habit of *making connections*. In a school day students move from one subject to another and sometimes from one teacher to another. Can they make connections between what was learned in English and what was learned in history? It happens spontaneously for some students, but most need some help with this. Teachers must cultivate connections in order to mediate this habit in their students' minds. The skill of making comparisons can be taught.

An easy way to start is by asking, "How are an apple and an orange alike? How are they different?" Begin questioning regularly for likenesses and differences in objects, themes, people. As you do, you begin moving your students up to second- and third-story intellects. They begin to make associations and before you know it they are aiming for the skylight.

A second habit of mind to develop is the *desire to give an oral response*. This innate inclination to respond, elaborate, and question is built by a sensitive teacher who clearly explains to students the importance of oral language and faithfully draws it from even the most reluctant learners at every opportunity. Openly valuing student contributions opens doors for further dialogue. Sometimes a one-on-one talk with a quiet, nonverbal student can encourage and inspire speech in a group setting.

A third habit of mind is believing that *we don't just learn from the teacher* but from one another as well. As the teacher mediates the group discussions it is important to affirm contributions such as, "Sue, you helped me to understand that idea better. Thank you." Or "This group has done some terrific thinking."

Finally, the most important habit of mind to establish for every student is the knowledge that *intellectual abilities can grow, flourish, and become stronger each day*. Praise progress, value the third-story responses, but particularly take them to the skylight, that place where they transcend the ideas of the teacher. Our friend Aesop seemed to understand that.

The Fox and the Lion

A fox who had never seen a lion one day met one, and was so terrified of the sight of him that he was ready to die with fear. After a time he met him again, and was still rather frightened but not nearly so much as he had been when he met him first. But when he saw him for the third time he was so far from being afraid that he went up to him and began to talk to him as if he had known him all his life.

As you begin to use the methods you are learning they will soon become very comfortable and your students will become comfortable with them. The fear you may have first felt as the fox did with the lion will diminish as you use them again and again. And your students will become less afraid of making oral responses as you set a respectful tone for all sincere ideas. Make it your goal to begin training oral speech so that it is clear, concise, and understandable. It is helpful to have a dictionary close by to check word meanings. The development of a strong vocabulary is a by-product of mediation and Socratic questioning. Mark Twain said:

Use the right word and not its second cousin.

REFLECTION

As we move beyond rote learning—that is, simply memorizing the content that will appear on the next test—we begin to discover that learning how to learn adds a motivational dimension to our development of three-story intellects. Students will begin to want to learn for its own sake. And so will we. By the way, have you read any good books lately? My emphasis is on *good*. Your vocabulary and syntax will stimulate your students'. Pick up a classic. Do you remember when you last read one of the really great books? Our literary ancestors in England gave us more than Churchill. An excellent book to read aloud to students is *Oliver Twist*. As you read such fine classics and those from other countries translated into English you will find your own language skills strengthened. Reading aloud builds memory too—which is the subject of our next chapter.

CHAPTER SEVEN

MOVING BEYOND MEMORIZATION

''Teachers can only be teachers when there are students
who want to be students.
Without a question, an answer is experienced as manipulation.
Without a struggle, help is considered as interference.
Without the desire to learn, the offer to teach
is easily felt as oppression.''

HENRI NOUWEN

WE CONTINUE to imagine a classroom filled with eager learners. Students ask questions and reflect upon the comments of their peers. They are developing intellectual curiosity and growing in their ability to reason, respond, and remember. Worksheets have reduced in number and preparation for the end-of-the-year testing has taken on a very different form. As students are becoming competent in learning how to learn, there is less emphasis on memorization of facts and more on oral dialogue. The teacher has grown more confident and competent also, even daring to believe that the test results this year will be better than ever. But what is the role of memorization in the transformation of thinking? Does it assist in developing the ability to learn? Read the following statement. Do you agree?

> **One of the primary goals of education is to help students retain and retrieve information.**

On the surface it seems reasonable, but I wonder if you have taken exception, as I do, to the word *primary*. Are retaining and retrieving simply information in, information out, so that once achieved our educational goals have been met? I am afraid many teachers and policymakers feel an undue sense of comfort when students are able to repeat what the text contains or what the teacher has told them. Surely, true education is about more than that. So what role does memorization play? We need to make a distinction between memorization and memory. This chapter's title, "Moving Beyond Memorization," suggests that there is some merit in the task of memorizing. As we dig deeper we will find that the complex arena of memory holds hidden treasures. Let's take a closer look.

MEMORY SYSTEMS

It is important to understand the different kinds of memory that contribute to thinking and learning. As we've already seen, our cognitive abilities are dynamic, not static. Researchers are discovering that memory is not found in just one part of the brain, but in many. In fact, the brain seems to be continually re-creating itself and memory is part of that re-creation. There are several kinds of memory. Let's briefly review them.

- *Working memory:* Our brains were designed to handle many pieces of information at once. That is how multitasking happens. If the information that comes into our brain through our senses is not acted upon—that is, stored somewhere—it will disappear in about twenty seconds. Meaningful connections need to be made. Sound familiar?

- *Semantic memory:* This is the type of memory we seem most concerned about in many classrooms. It consists of facts obtained through rote and drill. In other words, it is the *"what to learn,"* or content. These pieces of isolated information have limited connection to long-term memory unless strategies to remember them are taught. Even the strategies can fall off the memory screens if meaningful connections are not made.

- *Episodic memory:* This is the memory we tap into when we ask students to connect to their prior experience. It is also called *event memory* and must be drawn from the well of long-term memory. Again, it requires making connections.

- *Procedural memory:* The memory for physical routines such as driving, typing, or riding a bike demonstrates this kind of motor memory that becomes automatic over time. Handwriting falls into this category, and the dismal state of handwriting in our schools today reflects that many are not building these circuits.

- *Emotional memory:* All learning is affected by emotions, either positively or negatively. When students learn through positive emotions the memory of the lessons moves more quickly into long-term storage. Information taught when students are embarrassed, stressed, or angry has little chance of finding its way into long-term memory.

- *Long-term memory:* This is the strategic place from which we operate in thinking and learning. It is from here that we draw our language and experiences to build new cognitive circuits. We recall what we know and begin to assimilate what we have just learned. This highly networked area of the brain must have an ordered filing system to be able to store and retrieve.

STOPANDTHINK

How would you describe your memory? Is your memory for facts better than your memory for people or places? Is emotional memory a strong connector for you? What about procedural or working memory?

We are beginning to see how memory fits into the intelligence arena. It plays a role, certainly, but one of facilitator rather than command central. So, if we build memory resources are we building cognitive competency? That depends on whether that which is memorized has meaning for us. As a result of memorization are we moving students toward the skylight or simply putting stairs in place for them to climb? Let's do some memory work of our own. Come back in time with me, and as I continue my story try to remember yours.

MAKING MEMORIES

New orders came to this young navy family. We would leave Norfolk, Virginia, for San Diego. Lieutenant Ralph Hopkins was to be the executive officer aboard a fleet tug headed for the Far East. I would go with him, but only as far as California, where we would find an apartment and then say good-bye for six months. I had begun teaching third grade in Virginia and was, truthfully, quite relieved to be leaving it. The students were impossible to teach. Behavior problems that I could hardly imagine made each day a nightmare. When our orders came I did a little happy dance. Navy orders trumped teaching contracts. Little did I know how terribly lonely those six months would be. Emotional memories still linger.

In order to survive the agony of separation, I decided to become a permanent substitute. That meant I would need to be available to teach any class at any time. It was a large school district. These California students had never heard "Yes, ma'am" or "No, ma'am." They particularly loved a game called "Let's Confuse the Substitute." On many occasions they traded name cards or sat in the wrong seats. My working memory died daily. I began to seriously question my choice of occupation. Each evening I would come home to my lonely one-placemat meal and dread the early-morning phone call that would take me to yet another hostile classroom.

Then a permanent third grade position opened up. At least it brought some stability. Or did it? I found myself in the midst of the latest California innovation: moveable walls. My class was made up mostly of Mexican American students from poor families. I would just manage to get this large class settled into the next activity when it would be time to move the walls to form new groups with new classes in the middle of the building. Six classrooms used this creative space, and when the walls moved the result was instant chaos.

One day the boys in my class decided to surprise me by bringing five large tarantulas from the playground into the room; they were crawling all over their arms. To say that I was terrified would be an understatement. The emotional memories made during my first years of teaching were a virtual roller coaster. Yet, for better or worse, each is deeply embedded in my long-term memory. There were good moments, of course. Once, while substituting, I was told by the principal that the parents were so pleased with what I had taught their children that they wanted me to be their permanent teacher. Another gold coin for my pocket—they were few and far between in those days. Then, my beloved returned and our orders once again sent us back to the East Coast, this time to Newport, Rhode Island. My teacher's heart was battered but still beating.

LET'S GET PERSONAL

What about your early days in the classroom? Are your memories painful or pleasant? Focus for a moment on the pleasant ones and try to identify what made them so. I suspect it was because you sensed real learning happening, not just memorization of facts, though that is a part of learning.

When students are able to parrot back to you their surface knowledge, they are in the bottom story of the house. When their knowledge becomes meaningful they move into a whole new cognitive dimension. We might say that their neural architecture changes and they find themselves headed for the skylight. Let's dig more deeply into the memory system.

MEMORY TYPES

There is a difference between what scientists call natural memory and the work of memorization. Compare, for example, memorizing a list of words with remembering what we ate for dinner last night. The latter usually takes little effort (try it yourself) and the former some sort of repetition or concerted effort. Much ordinary information is retained seemingly effortlessly in our memories, and we can call upon it at any time. For example, you can most likely quickly recall events of your wedding day or the birth of your first child. Yet you did not have to study those things to remember them. Education seems to generally disregard the huge reservoirs of natural memory that students have for the events of life. The interaction of the two memory systems, natural and specific, has been studied and has tremendous relevance as we teach students how to learn, not just what to learn. Are you ready for some surprises?

The type of memory that involves focused storage is called *taxon memory,* according to Caine and Caine (1991), from the word *taxonomy* or list. There are many taxon systems, such as procedures, categories, and word lists. The pervasive characteristic that they all require is rehearsal. This can be illustrated by an Information Processing Model.

Study this model for a moment. As information such as a telephone number reaches our sensory register, we focus on a few signals that seem important, such as grouping numbers to recall them more easily. Interestingly, seven chunks of information (the exact content of a telephone number) is normal cognitive capacity. I wonder if the designers of our telephone systems knew that.... (How can I find out? I am headed for the Internet! Remember to wonder!)

The signals, or numbers, in the first stage of rehearsal go into immediate memory (see again Figure 7.1). If we rehearse them well enough, they land in long-term memory. We all have had times when we thought our telephone number was firmly entrenched in long-term memory only to be taken by surprise when asked to produce it. Our response is usually, "I don't call it very often!" Rehearsal is the key factor in taxon memory.

Taxon learning depends on extrinsic motivation. We must have a reason or desire to remember the data. Learning information for a test falls into this category. If you want to pass, you need to learn it. These taxon or list memories seem to be learned or fixed in a way that makes them resistant to change. They can become structures in the mind so firmly entrenched that they prohibit

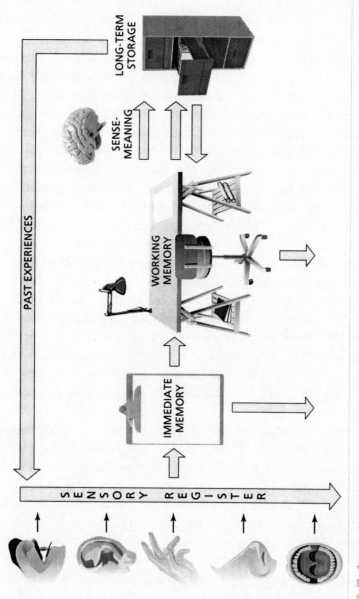

FIGURE 7.1. The Information Processing Model

application in any new context. For example, students learn the spelling words from a list to pass a test but then cannot spell them correctly when writing a paper.

I cannot recall "The Leak in the Dike" by Phoebe Cary today. I have not recently rehearsed it, and though it might be present somewhere in my long-term memory, I cannot access it. In order to embed it for my performance I must have repeated it thousands of times. Yet today I have only a vague appreciation for the little girl in Holland who saved her village. The poem that I memorized as a child has become for me a long-term memory of an event.

Knowledge stored in the taxon systems does not transfer easily. Taxon memories are relatively isolated. An example is the established memory of driving a car, a stable entity that can be called on and used in a fairly predictable manner. However, that skill does not transfer to piloting an airplane. Much of what is stored in taxon memory is not initially meaningful. Think of the task of learning the alphabet by young children. The memory is there, but not the meaning. Take that into a sixth-grade class where a student will list the facts required to pass the test but have little or no idea of their meaning. Taxon memory has its limitations.

The second type of memory is called *locale memory*. Everything that happens to us in life happens in space, the kind we walk around in every day. We are continually operating in a very rich physical context that we learn to navigate, whether it is a furniture store or a new city. We constantly create and test spatial maps that give us information about our surroundings. I have a daughter who can go into a store, select the most wonderful bargain hanging on a rack, and in ten minutes complete her shopping trip! She is motivated by bargains, but there is something else at work here. Even though she has not previously seen that object on sale, from past experience she knows how to navigate a store and select an item from among many others.

Think about the last time you were in an airport. Even if you have never been in that airport before, past experience with airports kicks in. You remember that there are information boards, recall that all airports have food vendors and rest rooms, and remember the lines, smells, and sounds of airports that make them familiar. As we navigate through space we are continually monitoring a great deal of sensory information. We automatically form long-term memories of events and places without deliberately trying to. This is what distinguishes taxon memory from locale memory. Every one of us has a spatial or locale memory system, and its capacity is virtually unlimited.

Locale memories are almost always relationship-oriented specifically to where we are in space. They are records of ongoing life events, whether a trip to Hawaii or time spent reading a good book last night. These spatial maps seem to form very quickly, in contrast to the time it takes to memorize a list. When we visit a friend's home we pick up an immediate sense of the layout of the room we are in that will stay with us after we leave without any effort or rehearsal on our part. Updating these maps is continuous and virtually effortless. We are constantly comparing our present surroundings with similar past surroundings.

These memories are open-ended and flexible. Novelty, curiosity, and expectation motivate the making of these locale memories. We expect the world to be a particular way because of the preliminary maps and memories we form. Anything novel or different immediately gains our attention. The brain continues to find patterns and endeavors to make sense of the world. In other words, this memory is always "on" during our waking hours due to continual sensory input.

Locale memory is not just limited to physical space. We also have mental maps of information that fall into this category of memory. For example, we have a particular religious persuasion, or not. Both require a map. Our political positions form an interconnected pattern that shapes our beliefs but is relatively open to adding new information beyond the strict memorization of a list. In other words, we are constantly reevaluating and re-forming these mental maps because they tend to be more flexible than the information in taxon memory.

So how do these two memory systems interface to affect learning? Obviously, the locale system has more megabytes than the taxon system. However, these bits of information must be accessible through meaningful connections. Consider this:

We teach either to the memory or to the understanding.

Do you agree? Is it either or, or both? Can we capture that useful locale memory in order to enhance the taxon memory? And where does understanding fit into our new paradigm? Here is where the concept of the importance of connections serves us well. Remember our quick and easy definition of intelligence from Chapter One: the ability to make connections.

We also need to remember that intelligence is not constant or static but wonderfully open to change throughout a lifetime. This means that if you or some of your students have poor memories, we can change the *state* of their learning problems because difficulty with memory functioning is not a *trait* like blue eyes or red hair. Again, let's rehearse the formal definition of intelligence proposed by Professor Feuerstein (2007): "Intelligence is more correctly defined as the continuous changing state of an individual best reflected in the way that individual is able to use previous experiences to adapt to new situations" or "the ability to learn from what has been learned."

PRACTICAL APPLICATION

Now let's return to the significant role of the mediator in producing cognitive change. Taxon and locale memory may be likened to a GPS system and a map. The GPS gives you the route (taxon); the map (locale) is the larger system into which the GPS fits. The mediator uses both the lists stored in memory and the exploratory elements of a map to build intellectual competence.

It is true that many of the methods used in schools today predispose the brain to rely heavily on taxon memory. This shuts down map learning because maps are always complex and personal. It is far easier to measure taxon knowledge than to venture into the unknown beyond the facts. For this creates disequilibrium in both teacher and learner. However, it is the creation of disequilibrium that opens up the how-to-learn circuits. A competent mediator, which many teachers are without realizing it, can incorporate both memory systems to the highest advantage. Let's take a look at how this is done through a sample lesson (text taken from "The History Place," 2008).

The Text

The Irish Potato Famine

Beginning in 1845 and lasting for six years, the potato famine killed over a million men, women, and children in Ireland and caused another million to flee the country.

Ireland in the mid-1800s was an agricultural nation, populated by eight million persons who were among the poorest in the western world. Only about a quarter of the population could read and write. Life expectancy was short, just 40 years for men. The Irish married quite young—girls at 16, boys at 17 or 18—and tended to have large families, although infant mortality was also quite high.

A British survey in 1835 found half of the rural families in Ireland living in single-room, windowless mud cabins that did not have chimneys. The people lived in small communal clusters spread out around the beautiful countryside. Up to a dozen persons lived inside a cabin, sleeping in straw on the bare ground, sharing the place with the family's pig and chickens. In some cases, mud cabin occupants were actually the dispossessed descendants of Irish estate owners. It was not uncommon for a beggar in Ireland to mention that he was in fact the descendant of an ancient Irish king.

By the 1800s, the potato had become the staple crop in the poorest regions. More than three million Irish peasants subsisted solely on the vegetable, which is rich in protein, carbohydrates, minerals, and vitamins. It is possible to stay healthy on a diet of potatoes alone. Irish peasants were actually healthier than peasants in England or Europe where bread, far less nutritious, was the staple food.

The famine began quite mysteriously in September 1845 as leaves on potato plants suddenly turned black and curled, and then rotted, seemingly the result of a fog that had wafted across the fields of Ireland. The cause was actually an airborne fungus originally transported in the holds of ships traveling from North America to England.

As the famine worsened the Irish in the countryside began to live off wild blueberries, nettles, turnips, seaweed, roots, and grass. Fish remained out of reach in water too deep for the small fishing boats. Making matters worse the winter of 1846–47 became the worst in living memory as one blizzard after another buried homes in snow up to their roofs. The potato blight affected all of Europe, but the only famine was in Ireland.

The Lesson

Bring a potato to class. Ask a student to put it into a category (vegetable) and name a few other vegetables that are similar to a potato. Remember, this is building skills of comparison. Discuss ways in which potatoes can be prepared and have the students identify their favorites. This discussion engages the locale memory that takes no energy to retrieve from long-term memory, partly because it involves taste, a strong memory trigger. Let's suppose one student named mashed potatoes as a favorite. Tap the taxon memory by asking for a description of the procedures needed to go from raw potato to mashed potato. You are setting the two kinds of memory on active mode as you go into the lesson.

TEACHER: Ryan, have you ever been hungry?

STUDENT: Yes, last night before dinner.

TEACHER: Can you explain what it feels like?

STUDENT: My stomach growls and I get grumpy.

TEACHER: Ann, how would you define the word "famished"?

STUDENT: Very, very hungry.

TEACHER: Good. James, what do you think a famine is?

Work on precision and accuracy in language—review the dictionary definition prior to the lesson so that you can direct students in verbal expression. The dictionary definition is "an extreme scarcity of food." Be sure these terms are clarified through questioning a few students on their meanings.

As you lead students to understand the seriousness of a famine, have them discuss what the results of such a disaster would be, as well as the causes. Have them imagine that they are walking through a land where there is famine. What would they see? Discuss places that have famine today. You may have visuals or ask them to sketch what such a place might look like. You are stimulating locale memory here, a strong connector to long-term memory requiring little effort or rehearsal.

In order to connect geographically, have them find Ireland on an unlabeled world map. Give each student a copy and have a prize for the first to locate and outline it. Then have them check their answers for accuracy. Ask what they know about the country. Memory of events or locale memory will be strongest in those who have visited Ireland, but it can also be triggered by a film or book read about Ireland. Solicit some experiences and be ready to share your knowledge or experience of Ireland.

Put up a transparency of the Irish potato famine text, revealing only the first paragraph. Mediate their learning by asking the following questions:

- According to our definition of the word *famine,* what do you think a potato famine is?

- I am asking myself a question as I read this; are you? (In the absence of their questions, model yours.) I am wondering why an extreme scarcity of potatoes caused a famine. Didn't the people have other food? Let's read on.

Have students turn to the person next to them and read the next three paragraphs aloud, taking turns, to draw some conclusions about why not having potatoes caused a famine. Oral, quiet reading builds inner language for some learners better than silent reading. While they are still working as partners, have them make a list of reasons.

Finally, have students offer reasons for the famine before silent reading of the last two paragraphs. This interactive oral language–based activity goes well beyond memorization. It builds intellectual capacity for both the teacher and the students.

Since we have been discussing the importance and relative significance of food, let's close this chapter with a fable that can help your students make some connections.

The Town Mouse and the Country Mouse

 A town mouse and a country mouse were acquaintances, and the country mouse one day invited his friend to come and see him at his home in the fields. The town mouse came and they sat down to dinner of barleycorns and roots, the latter of which had a distinctly earthy flavor. The fare was not much to the taste of the guest and presently he broke out with, "My poor dear friend, you live here no better than the ants. Now you should just see how I fare! My larder is a relative horn of plenty. You must come and stay with me, and I promise you, you shall live on the fat of the land."

So when he returned to town he took the country mouse with him and showed him a larder containing flour and oatmeal and figs and honey and dates. The country mouse had never seen anything like it, and sat down to enjoy the luxuries his friend provided. But before they had well begun, the door of the larder opened and someone came in. The two mice scampered off and hid themselves in a narrow and exceedingly uncomfortable hole. Presently, when all was quiet, they ventured out again; but someone else came in and off they scuttled again. This was too much for the visitor. "Good-bye," said he. "I'm off. You live in the lap of luxury, I can see, but you are surrounded by dangers; whereas at home I can enjoy my simple dinner of roots and corn in peace."

See if you can develop a list of questions that would stimulate comparisons within this fable. List the similarities and differences in each. For example, list the ways the town and country mice were alike and different. Is there a modern story that parallels this one? Many of your students will be familiar with the story of Ratatouille, the famous cartoon French cook. Lead them into a comparison of Aesop's fable and the modern one. A question you could ask is who was Ratatouille most like, the town mouse or the country mouse, and why. Allow for differences in opinion here.

REFLECTION

Making connections is one of the most powerful how-to-learn tools. Use it often. Consider how many possible opportunities you may have to draw comparisons during a given day. Are you beginning to have some preliminary thoughts? We call those your *inner voices,* and they are the subject of our next chapter.

CHAPTER EIGHT

THOSE INNER VOICES

"He that is indeed wise does not bid you to enter the house of his wisdom but rather leads you to the threshold of your own mind."

M. MASTOPIERI, KEYNOTE ADDRESS, LEARNING
DISABILITIES ASSOCIATION CONFERENCE

WE MUST now drill down into some neuropsychological constructs in order to understand the role of inner language in the learning process. This ability to talk to oneself inwardly is a uniquely human trait. Some have called it a God-given "conscience" or "the little men on each shoulder influencing toward good or evil." Regardless of our beliefs on this matter, inner speech is a contributor to efficient learning. The important question for us as we consider teaching students how to learn is this: How can we build inner speech in the classroom?

Think of the last time you lost your keys. What did you do? Chances are your inner language became overt as you began to speak audibly to yourself. It may have gone something like this, "Oh, no, now where did I put them? I can't believe I am so stupid, today of all days. Okay, let me think, what did I do as soon as I came into the house . . . ?" We have all caught ourselves speaking aloud under stress. Somehow bringing that covert language into the open assists us in solving the problem.

Before heading into some deeper neuropsychological waters, let's do some continued reflection of our journeys toward competence and confidence as educators. If we are not in those places it is doubtful we can lead students there.

LET'S GET PERSONAL

Before reading my story, take a quick assessment of your competence level. Have you been feeling a bit more intelligent as we have journeyed together? What about your confidence? Is it improving? Confidence usually precedes competence. Let's move ever more surely toward our own skylights.

NEW LANGUAGES

My professional development was about to be interrupted by motherhood. Giving birth to two daughters within five years was a most enriching experience. My sincere love of children found a new expression as I gazed blissfully at my own. The call to teach took on a whole new perspective. I loved every moment of the learning I experienced parenting my young children. It was a different kind of schoolhouse but a most rewarding one.

The U.S. Navy continued to move us from East Coast to West Coast, with our growing daughters in tow. We learned to adapt and not put roots down too deeply. During this time my husband and I took nine weeks of Thai language instruction in preparation for our orders to Bangkok. I learned what it meant to think in another language. Our youngest daughter was born in Thailand, so she began life with bilingual circuits, and our eldest became bilingual at age five with much greater ease than it took her parents to acquire the language. Cognitive modifiability does have its windows!

My memory of those days is that my inner speech was strengthened by having to process two languages. Hearing another language spoken reinforced my native tongue rather than confuse it. I remember walking by the open air Thai schools and hearing large groups of children reciting their school work in unison. I wondered if this recitation was helping them remember or think or neither. And I began to long to return to the classroom.

This happened in a most interesting way. Soon after our return from Thailand we were given new orders to London. Our daughters entered the village infant school in Stoke Poges, Buckinghamshire, and I volunteered to become a remedial teacher, just to help out. Little did I know that this decision would start me on a monumental professional journey that has not yet ended. Our family became English for six years—all but Ralph, who worked with Americans and so retained his native tongue. My inner speech took on an English accent. It happened rather spontaneously and without effort on my part. It was not just the speech but the behaviors that changed. I was beginning to think and act like my English friends. But the reality of the differences between us became starkly obvious the first day I walked into the classroom.

I was thrown into the lion's den when presented with a group of nineteen remedial learners. At this point in my professional career I had never even heard the term "learning disabilities." Nothing I had studied or experienced as a teacher had prepared me for this. These little lions' mouths were wide open. To make matters worse they located my class in the library next to the headmistress's office. I soon learned this formidable woman could hear every word. One day, Duncan, a ragamuffin little boy with a cockney accent, blurted out, "I don't believe in God." In seconds Eve O'Sullivan bounded through the door, picked up Duncan by the collar and said, "What do you mean you don't believe in God?" My own faith was hanging in the balance.

It was sink or swim. . . . No workbooks or worksheets were used in the English schools, only composition books into which students wrote their daily news in their journals with any other assignments. There was no specific reading instruction; instead, each child read aloud daily to the teacher in a look-say approach. I was sinking. What was I to do? They did not even have reading groups, the mainstay of American reading instruction. Besides that, my speech seemed unintelligible to my students. As I gave them an instruction they would look at me in an odd way and try not to laugh. I was later told that my voice reminded them of Kermit the frog, whom they heard regularly on American television. Obviously my oral language was not my strong suit here.

Inner speech by way of executive functioning kicked in. I began spending hours each evening making plans and materials, drawing from my long-term memory. Creating a curriculum from scratch was not something my college degree had prepared me for. I was in for the ride of my life.

INNER SPEECH

Each of us operates with a more or less intact system of covert language. We have been learning it from birth. Words form our thoughts in a fascinating abbreviated fashion that we are most often unaware of. Yet this inner language provides the basis for cognitive reasoning, self-regulation, and problem solving. Children with underdeveloped inner speech have been found to be at risk for learning problems.

According to Vygotsky, oral language directs and develops thinking processes. *Thought and Language* (1994) explains this vital connection. His theory on the development of private, inner speech is the position most accepted by professionals today.

> *Inner speech:* **Speech uttered aloud by children that is addressed either to the self or to no one in particular.**

Early speech of this sort in a child usually is accompanied by specific actions. As it matures it functions as a form of self-guidance. For example, the child is playing with blocks on the floor. He says quietly, "I put the red block by the blue one to make this train." Gradually, as speech becomes progressively more private or internalized, the child's actions become increasingly under his cognitive control. Finally, the outer speech of a child goes underground and becomes completely covert, consolidating into thought patterns that feed both memory and comprehension.

It is this inner speech that we as educators can strengthen as we teach children through oral dialogue in the classroom. The mediator brings the hidden or covert speech out into the open so that it can be strengthened, only to become covert again in the working memory.

For example, you might ask a student what he knows about a frog. His response: "I think it lives in water, um, like an amphibian." You will work with him orally, with that sentence guiding the development of his final sentence in terms of clarity. At first you may say, "Can you say what you know more clearly?" If there is no response, suggest that he begin his sentence with, "I know a frog is an amphibian because. . ." Lead (do not tell) the student to consider that it is an amphibian because it can live both on land and in water. Draw those thoughts from him. This is true mediation; you are helping him frame and focus his knowledge into clear oral language.

The final sentence, crafted collaboratively, would sound something this: "A frog is an amphibian because it begins its life in the water as a tadpole and then lives the rest of its life on land." When the student produces that sentence he is building both his oral language and his ability to think more clearly. Inner speech improves not just for this student but for all who are listening to the dialogue.

Language pulls cognition out of our mouths. Weak, random oral speech usually reflects weak, random thinking. As we strengthen the speech we strengthen the thinking. Later in this chapter we will discover how this works in a classroom setting. Let's dig a bit deeper into the theory by examining the role of executive functioning.

EXECUTIVE FUNCTION

The term *executive function* refers to the brain's ability through inner speech to regulate ideas, plans, and intentions that are purposeful and directed across time. These important cognitive functions are located in the highly integrated frontal lobe of the brain. Executive functions are rather like the things executives do: make decisions, plan reports, sustain focus on a project, or comprehend a theory. They are also required in school, so they need to be built beginning in about fourth grade.

Executive functioning has been called the "orchestra leader" of the brain because it guides all cognitive systems to work together to produce a well-integrated response—or concert. The key is that executive functioning is internal, not external. A teacher can never serve as the child's orchestra leader or become his frontal lobe. Yet many of us try.

Human language, according to theories advanced by Barkley (1997), has unique properties related to the work of the prefrontal cortex, or executive functioning. In a strategic way, language skills develop and support verbal working memory. This working memory can be described as the individual's ability to keep one or more items of information in mind in the absence of an external cue (such as visual input) and use that information to produce a response. Take another look at our Information Processing Model in Chapter Seven. Can you see how inner language must move information from the sensory input channels into long-term memory? It was the inner language of executive functioning that I used in England when I created my remedial curriculum from scratch. I searched my long-term files and built something new from what I found there.

Further, according to Barkley, the process of developing private speech is a major contributor to the development of self-control. In fact, Barkley would argue that the executive functions permit human self-regulation. Those with ADHD seem to have greater difficulty using their inner language to reflect on their actions before making a decision.

This difficulty in inhibiting behavior, or specifically, a weakness in inner speech, may better explain the problems of ADHD than specific attentional weaknesses. Most students with ADHD can attend very well to something that interests them. But their inner speech is not well established, meaning that they cannot talk themselves out of or through a situation.

The capacity to inhibit or delay responses involves the ability to refer back in time and look to the future before deciding to act. Inner speech plays a significant role in the ability to reflect, ponder, and decide.

Another property of inner language for executive functioning is the ability to separate the emotional component from the cognitive. When a person can purposefully delay a response, it gives the inner language time to travel through other information circuits in the brain, creating greater objectivity and reason. It could well mean the difference between reacting and responding in an emotionally charged situation. The logo Professor Feuerstein uses on all his instruments is: "Just a moment, let me think." Curbing impulsivity is a cognitive skill that can be developed through the use of inner language.

ACTIVE WORKING MEMORY

Internal speech often plays a role in active working memory. Self-directed speech provides a means for reflection, problem solving, self-questioning, and moral reasoning. Humans live with two languages, an inner and an outer one. We are constantly experimenting with and revising inner language when establishing cognitive beliefs or assertions. These inner structures are then transferred to outer language in the form of decisions or plans. Our own inner language is constantly under refinement, and in the spirit of cognitive modifiability the inner language of our students is wonderfully open to change. As is our own.

PRACTICAL APPLICATION #1

Given that inner language supports good thinking, which tools assess the inner language abilities of students? Let me suggest a place to start.

Put a single word on the board, a word that can be several parts of speech. Let's use the word *train*. Have students put all papers and pencils aside. They are to use only their minds for this one; no writing. Ask them to think of a definition for this word, not the first thought that comes into their minds but a thought explored and developed through their inner language. Preliminarily, you may need to model this thinking if you sense your class will struggle with this activity. You might say something like this:

> *When I think of the word* train *the first thought that comes to my mind is the vehicle or mode of transportation. I can picture a silver bullet train that I once traveled on. So I wonder if the first dictionary definition is, "a vehicle." But then, if I think more about it, I know there is a kind of wedding dress that has a* train

or a long part of the skirt that drags behind. Then, I can think of a third meaning of that word, to train *someone means to teach them something.*

If you sense that your class can handle the challenge, proceed without the modeling. Encourage them to think of as many meanings of that word as they can without writing them down. Have them hold their ideas in their heads or in their working memory. They will soon learn this term and become familiar with the way their brain works and improves. If you have a brain chart on the wall they may be interested to know that they are developing their frontal lobes through this activity.

As they manipulate ideas cognitively, have them center on what they think the most common use of the word is; that definition will be listed first in the dictionary. Ask them to use their inner speech to construct what the first dictionary definition is. Give them time to process.

Remember, they are using inner language to direct their thinking. That language may be weak and vulnerable. Be sensitive to those who find this difficult. There should be no oral language happening in the room right now, only inner speech. They may not realize that they are able to talk to themselves in their heads.

At this point, let students use their oral language to tell a partner their choice of the first meaning of train they think is listed in the dictionary. For example, they may say the first definition listed is "a vehicle." That would be my guess, but I have not looked it up yet. Be a learner with your students. Then, as a second activity, have them decide what part of speech their word is and why. Have them defend their choice to their partner.

Examples: My choice of "train" is:

- A noun because it names a thing

- A verb because it shows action

- An adjective because it describes something

Their oral speech must be clear and concise. Circulate so you can mediate unclear responses. According to their choice, have them give a clear, concise definition of the word, as might be found in the dictionary. Still, no writing has taken place. You are stretching the requirement on their active working memories and building their capacity for inner speech. The minute they write something down their brains no longer need to hold it. (By the way, my guess about the first dictionary definition of train was incorrect. You might be surprised at what it is. Look it up!)

Transition again to covert speech by asking them to think of an original sentence using their word as that specific part of speech. Again, no pencils. We are working on inner language in forming a sentence. See if they can refine their original thought, making their sentence sound better, all inside their heads. Encourage them to edit their sentence while it is still in their minds. Some may be able to visualize their sentence as if it was on the board, erasing and replacing words mentally.

When they are satisfied with their sentence tell them they can now pick up their pencils and see if they can write it just the way they arranged it in their heads. Then have them underline the word "train" and write its part of speech in parentheses at the end of the sentence. Have partners check one another and verbally correct each other.

These sentences are your first assessment of your students' inner language abilities. Have them date their papers and expect great improvement in the next few months as you work on this skill.

For fun, see how many parts of speech you found for this one word. Then and only then, look up the word *train* in a dictionary. Perhaps have a contest for the one finding it first. All students should have a dictionary handy in their desks and become competent in locating words quickly. Did anyone come up with the first dictionary definition exactly as it was stated? You will want to work toward precision in language using a standard Webster's dictionary. This activity will not only help students with vocabulary but also improve their thinking processes—their "how-to-learn" circuits—tremendously. Their search could lead into a delightful discovery of dictionary abbreviations and meaningful comparisons of the three primary parts of speech for the word *train*.

I would imagine that most students could identify the fact that this word could be either a noun or a verb. Did anyone think that it could also be an adjective? ("The train station was very busy this morning.") Have partners see if they can orally use it three different ways in a sentence. Written assignments could follow.

The power of this activity is its ability to build inner speech. When students must manipulate ideas without benefit of visual cues (that is, worksheets) they are creating neural circuits that are transferable to other activities. They learn how to learn, not just what. Yet, in the process, the what or content is also remembered. I would expect the three meanings of train might find their way to the dinner table that night, especially if they nailed the specific dictionary definition!

THE CASE FOR GRAMMAR

It was noted by Vygotsky that grammar is a subject considered by many to be of little practical use. When in life do we need to understand nouns and verbs? In fact, some schools have stopped teaching grammar. But consider Vygotsky's position (1994, pp. 183–184):

> *Grammar is a subject that seems to be of little practical use. Unlike other school subjects it does not give a child new skills. He conjugates and declines before he enters school. The opinion has even been voiced that school instruction in grammar could be dispensed with. We can only reply that our analysis clearly showed the study of grammar to be of paramount importance for the mental development of the child.*

These are strong words from one who understood the importance of the link between language and thinking. Let's try to unwrap some of the reasons for Vygotsky's statement.

The brain is designed to perceive and generate patterns. A cornerstone of the capacity to learn is the brain's ability to perceive what is alike, or what scientists call *instances of sameness*. Good thinkers are always connecting new learning to past knowledge and asking themselves, "How is this like that?" Struggling learners seem to have no inner voices telling them to make connections. They seem to see life in episodes; nothing connects to anything else. In order to support the recognition of sameness, categories need to be created.

The creation of distinct categories into which words fit provides a handy tool for recognizing similarities. Parts of speech have specific characteristics. Nouns name, verbs show action, adjectives describe. The brain loves order and design. Although parts of speech are an abstract concept in that they cannot be seen or touched, they build mental competency by their very nature, for they need to be manipulated by the mind not the hands.

Knowing how words can be categorized enhances flexibility of thinking and ease of expression, both oral and written. The labels (noun, verb, and so on) provide handy mental "drawers" for storage, to be opened at will. I recently asked my eleven-year-old grandson to tell me what part of speech the word *magically* is. He quickly went through the "drawers" in his mind, and after asking what the verb was in the sentence said, "It is an adverb because it describes the verb, appears." This is long-term storage at its best. The spontaneous question was asked him in late August, and his mind was definitely not on academics. This kind of thinking will serve him very well as he begins middle school next week.

The initial teaching of grammar is most effectively done orally, not with a workbook. Consider this approach.

PRACTICAL APPLICATION #2

Orally give a list of things (table, chair, boy, friend, city, country) and ask what category they could be put in. Explore the idea that they are *things* that can be given the name *noun*.

Write the list on the board and see if they notice that the nouns are in three categories. As they generate the words write *person*, *place,* and *thing* across the board and have them come up and put the words under the correct category. Then lead them to discover the definition of a noun. Interestingly, many high school students could benefit from a review like this before writing a composition.

A noun is a word that names *a person, place, or thing.* Have them repeat this definition to one another alternately, in pairs. Make sure they are emphasizing the word *names*. Now have them in their pairs take three to five minutes to generate as many nouns as they can think of while putting them under the correct categories. Have them create a three-column page with the categories Person, Place, and Thing written under the heading Nouns, with the definition just underneath. Give appropriate praise to the winning team.

Be sure to rehearse this definition often in the days following so that when you ask what part of speech a word is, the student answers, "Noun." It is not enough to say, "Good," and move on; ask the question, "*Why* is this a noun?" The student's response and correct defense of his answer should be, "Because it names a thing" (or a person or a place).

REFLECTION

Through this activity you are building strong inner language and taking the knowledge of parts of speech beyond memory into understanding. When a student can defend or prove her answer, she moves beyond the one-story intellect up to the second floor. Of course, our goal is to reach the third story with the skylight. The teaching of grammar is a tool that will help us get there. More about that in the next chapter. Let's close with a fable.

The Dog and His Reflection

 A dog was crossing a plank bridge over a stream with a piece of meat in his mouth when he happened to see his own reflection in the water. He thought it was another dog with a piece of meat twice as big, so he let go of his own and flew at the other dog to get the other piece. But of course, all that happened was that he got neither. For one was only a reflection and the other was carried away by the current.

This fable has great teaching power. Read it aloud to the class and have them picture what is happening. Then have one come to the board to illustrate the scene. Have another retell the story in her own words. Then see how many nouns they can recall from the story, just from their auditory memory. This builds inner language and active working memory.

Have a copy of the fable to hand out to groups of four. See which group can identify the correct number of nouns in the story. As they share their lists they must defend why each is a noun.

As always, see if your students can identify the lesson that Aesop was teaching. This opens the skylight.

CHAPTER NINE

POTENTIAL OR PROPENSITY?

''There is nothing more practical than a good theory.''
KURT LEWIN

125

FINDING PROPENSITY

There I was, in a tiny English village, trying desperately to teach struggling learners. My theory at that time was that these students had limited potential. Therefore, my best approach was to adjust the curriculum (that is, whatever I had created) downward for them. Surely, that would be the kindest thing to do—not expect very much so neither they nor I would be disappointed.

First, I had to learn the language. I found out that when I said "Tuesday" it brought the house down. My pronunciation sounded to them like "Toosday." Little polite titters were everywhere. Their more refined pronunciation of the word sounded to me like "Chyousday." I practiced hard in front of a mirror at night and began to feel as if I myself had a serious learning problem.

Where should I begin with nineteen six- to seven-year-olds who had no idea how to read, write, or spell? Daily I waited for Eve O'Sullivan to come through the door, screaming, "You can't do that!"

So I began with the most basic thing I could think of. I created a moveable alphabet. I spent hours each evening printing and cutting and placing in envelopes nineteen little alphabets. Since phonics instruction was not part of their experience, we would start there. It was magic! Before long my rather naïve theory that these students had limited potential was proven quite wrong. They were learning and so was I. It was time for me to develop a better theory.

POTENTIAL

What is the meaning of learning potential? We have already discussed that cognition is modifiable, that it is open to change under the right conditions and with the right mediation in the classroom. Now let's see how Webster's defines the term:

> *Potential:* **Existing in possibility; capable of development into actuality.**

This definition seems to imply limits, meaning it may or may not develop beyond just possibility. Admittedly, when we assess students in the classroom we look carefully at their prior and present performance. We mentally place them in a range of learning potential from low to high. It is what reading groups are all about. Teachers assign tasks or groups based on their assessment of the student's theoretical learning potential.

There is no question that there are a variety of learning styles, habits, and abilities present in every classroom. No two students are alike. At question is the teacher's ability to describe or evaluate a child's learning potential accurately. Rarely does a teacher see beyond current performance. We usually adjust our expectations downward, thinking that to be the kindest thing to do, as I did mentally with my nineteen remedial students. But our incorrect assessment of a child's learning potential can actually inhibit learning, both the child's and our own. I believe that even discussing the learning potential of a child can be a dangerous place to go. We easily underestimate both ourselves and others.

PROPENSITY

Let's consider an alternative term, and if I may propose, a new theory—that of learning propensity. Again let's go to Webster:

> *Propensity:* **A deeply ingrained and unusual longing; a natural inclination or preference.**

Now here is an interesting thought. If there is within every child, and I believe there is, a natural inclination toward learning, a propensity or a leaning toward understanding and knowledge, then what kills it? Certainly there are students who appear to have no desire to learn. But truly, have you ever seen a kindergarten child who was not filled with propensity? The sky is the limit for these little ones. Something seems to happen between kindergarten and later grades for many children that diminishes that natural, inherent desire to learn. It seems to me we ought to be asking the why question.

If, as we have discussed, intellectual abilities can be enhanced, why for some do they seem to deteriorate? It is important for every teacher to have a strong belief in the ability to change cognitive capabilities. But first we must understand the problem, and although we may not want to face it, we teachers may be a factor in their loss of the love of learning. How are we teaching?

We teach who we are and what we believe. Perhaps it is time for a moment's reflection:

STOPANDTHINK

Are you the kind of teacher who inspires reluctant learners? If so, reflect on your secrets, maybe even write them down. I suspect there are other teachers in your school who would love to know them. If you are fairly certain this is not a strength for you, ask another teacher in your school to let you observe her. This could be a great topic to discuss together in an afterschool in-service.

The good news continues to be our own cognitive modifiability as professionals. We can change our thinking and our methods. But we must be willing to embrace our own propensity and launch out into some unknown territory. Ruts are very comfortable. Can we agree to take a higher road?

Picture the trajectory that we have mentioned earlier, one that continues to rise skyward, toward the light and throughout the lifetime. This image presents a clear picture of propensity. We may need to examine our belief system carefully. Have we put ceilings on children's learning? Despite our content-driven curricula, I believe we have both the opportunity and the knowledge to motivate a child who has lost the desire to learn. If we can leave behind our unrealistic understanding of learning potential and move into the much more attractive concept of learning propensity, we will have taken a major step toward the skylight. Let's repeat this helpful saying:

> ### *Never* lower your expectations
> ### to the child's current level of functioning.

Always aim just higher, not unrealistically so as to cause frustration, but just above current functioning so as to inspire confidence.

BUILDING CONFIDENCE

Those who struggle with some aspect of learning tend to lack confidence in any new cognitive task. Consider how you feel about the subject of mathematics. Does it bring a groan, as I have heard in many teacher workshops, when I say, "Now let's do some math." If you like math, you probably cannot quite appreciate your colleagues' distress at even the suggestion of this subject. If this is you, fill in the blank with another subject that you have found or find difficult, such as grammar. It is important for us as educators to understand how our personal confidence level may limit our cognitive ability—or shall we say cognitive propensity? After all, our brains are wired to understand, so let's open them up.

Dislike of a particular subject can stem from a variety of sources. The teacher may not be very good at teaching it, or the students may not be willing to persevere through the hard places. Among students, processing weaknesses, such as auditory or visual difficulties, can inhibit understanding. We will touch on these later in the chapter. It is important to consider exactly what has interfered with the desire to learn. The propensity to learn is innate, so it has not disappeared. It remains hidden under the cloaks of misbehavior, frustration, apathy, and the terrible fear of failure. Fear and anxiety are powerful destroyers of the desire to learn.

PRACTICAL APPLICATIONS

I was recently asked to give a workshop to a large group of K–12 teachers who were preparing to begin their school year the next day. The morning speaker was just leaving as I arrived. I could see in the teachers' faces the strong desire to leave the workshop so they could prepare their classrooms for tomorrow. They were not motivated to hear yet another speaker drone on for three more hours. As we gathered after lunch and the last stragglers reluctantly took their seats, I began to feel overwhelmed by the task before me. I wished I could just let them go.

Reluctant learners have a way of deflating teacher confidence. I sent up a quick prayer and soldiered on. Though my confidence in myself was low, it was high in the material I had to present. In fact, I was excited about it and knew from past experience that I could get these teachers excited about it too. It didn't take long. They soon became actively engaged in the learning process; in fact, they contributed a great deal of information that I had not included in my notes or even thought of. At the end of the day they thanked me and told me how very practical the session had been for them. Maybe that is part of the secret in inspiring those who have a fragile desire to learn: make it practical.

In order to do this in your classroom, you need to know your students. What really matters to them? What do they love to do? Those things are confidence builders and every child needs to have or acquire at least one. If confidence is fragile, competence is often the casualty.

Mediating a Feeling of Competence

Being competent in a subject or task does not always equal *feeling* competent. Sometimes students need their competence mediated by an affirmation of their performance. For example, you might say: "What you have just done proves that you are a very competent learner." Students who have often been criticized either at home or in school tend to reject or devalue even the things they do well.

Two things need to happen in order to rebuild the propensity to learn. First, create situations where the learner can experience true competence. This competence should be acknowledged verbally, preferably in the hearing of their peers. Flattery, in contrast, is not helpful. Often teachers fall into the trap of saying continually, "That was very good," when in fact, it was not. Save your sincere praise for true affirmations and be specific in your comments, such as, "The strategic thinking you were able to explain on that tough math word problem was outstanding."

Second, help students appreciate and build on areas where competence exists but is fragile and undeveloped. They may not think they have competence in math, so mediate the feeling of competence through statements such as, "You are getting so much better at working long division. Let me show you a paper you did one month ago. I think you are using strategies much more effectively now. Talk me through how you did this problem."

Students should understand the fine line between mastery and competence. These are two phases of learning that are quite distinct and recognizable. *Mastery* indicates that the process or material has been overlearned to the point of automaticity. For example, you have mastered your multiplication tables to the point of automatic recall in any situation or with any multiple. A feeling of competence usually precedes, rather than follows, mastery. It can happen through "aha" moments due to the way the material was taught or through a conceptual understanding of why the concept works. If a student can demonstrate through manipulatives why $3 \times 4 = 12$, she is reflecting competence in the learning process. Figure 9.1 provides a visual depiction of how multiplication works. If students are not able to illustrate the process, they are probably operating from memory rather than understanding.

Competency has more to do with *how* to learn, or the process. It is what the teacher has the greatest power to influence. Mastery, in contrast, is the *what*. This is another way of stating the concepts of fluid and crystallized intelligence.

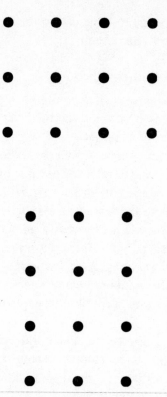

FIGURE 9.1. The How of Multiplication

The teacher-mediator must carefully discern the student's own perception of her competence. It may or may not be accurate. "I am not good at math" may be a false assumption.

Practical Application #1

Suppose a student is presented with a word problem, the most difficult task in mathematics for all learners. The first comment is, "Oh no, I hate these." The worst thing you can do is ask everyone to work it silently. Working it together as a class provides a great opportunity for building competence. Let's suppose that you, the teacher, not the textbook, have created problems based on specific interests you know your students have. They should be timely and reflective of the culture in which the students are immersed but which they often feel detached from. Michael Phelps astounded the world by winning eight gold medals at the 2008 Olympics. You can find data on such events easily on the Internet, making the quick creation of a word problem an activity that will build *your* confidence and competence. For high school students, have them create the problems. Do not wait for the textbooks to catch up with current events. They never will.

Read the word problem orally. (I just made this one up from the data so I know you can too!) It is helpful to have small, individual whiteboards for students to use during this activity. Each student should have a copy of the problem, just one problem at a time, not an entire sheet that may seem overwhelming.

Word Problem

> On August 12, Michael Phelps set a world record in the 200m freestyle with a time of 1:42.96. On August 16, he set another world record in the 100m butterfly with a time of 50.58. Which is his faster stroke? Prove it by your calculations.

First, clarify all abbreviations and be sure the students have read the numbers correctly. Introduce the idea of a strategy using TAPS.

T: What does the problem *tell* us? Lead students to list data on their whiteboards.

> 200m freestyle: 1:42.96 (Encourage abbreviation of *free* and *fly*.)

> 100m butterfly: 50.58

> Be sure you have discussed what the numbers mean and have a student read the time as "One minute forty two seconds and ninety six hundredths of a second." Data should be put on boards with the decimal places in alignment.

A: What does the problem ask us? Which stroke is faster?

> This should be a group discussion about the two strokes, which the students think is faster, and why. No figuring should be happening yet, only discussion.

P: What process are you going to use to find the answer?

> Again this should be a group discussion about the four processes of addition, subtraction, multiplication, and division. Have them record on their whiteboards the sign or signs for the process or processes they think they will use to solve the problem. Have them defend their choice to a partner.

S: How many steps will you need to take?

> Have them use their inner language to think through the process and use no overt language during this phase. Once they think they have a number of steps, have them put the number on their board and then compare with their partner.

Before they solve the problem, have one student orally suggest the first step. It may go something like this. "One race was 100m and the other was 200m. I think you need to estimate how long it would take Michael to swim 200m with the butterfly stroke. Even though there are some other things to consider, we need to be able to compare the two races. To do that you double his 100m time, or multiply by two. Then, subtract the smaller time from the larger. So I think we have two steps with two different processes. But we will have to do some conversions of seconds to minutes in order for the problems to line up."

Once this oral discussion has taken place—and you may need to guide it to keep it on the right track—have your students work the problems independently. Let those who finish early and correctly give some guidance to others. This is one way their whiteboards could look, but there are other ways to reach the same answer:

$$
\begin{array}{ccc}
50{:}58 & 101.16 & 1{:}42.96 \\
\times 2.00 & -60.00 & -1{:}41.16 \\
\hline
101{:}16 & 41.16 & 1.80
\end{array}
$$

Notice there are no labels yet. Have someone read the answers, giving labels as she explains the calculations. Once the final answer is given, we still have to answer the question that the problem asked. Which stroke was faster?

Michael's butterfly stroke is faster than his freestyle. Are you surprised? To inspire intellectual curiosity suggest that it might have something to do with Michael's physical build. They can find out some fascinating things about this for homework by looking it up online.

If just one word problem is mediated this way, the competence of all learners is increased much more than having students silently do a page of problems on a worksheet. And I suspect that because you found and wrote the problem out, your own cognitive competence was enhanced. Remember:

A brain once stretched by a new idea never regains its original shape.

More Practical Applications

Since we are on the subject of mathematics, let's discuss some ideas for building competence that may be used throughout the day at various intervals, not just during math class.

- Foundational to a conceptual understanding of our base ten system is what we call "partners to 10." What two numbers when added together equal 10? The teacher calls out the number 7 and a student replies 3. Then she calls out 5; the reply is 5. These partners should be overlearned to automaticity. Give one set of dice to two students and have them shake one at a time, with the other student stating the partner to the number shown on the first one. This is a great confidence builder.

- Once these are mastered have them say the next highest 10 to 57. The answer is 60. They have to apply and explain orally their knowledge of partners ("3 is 7's partner to 10 so the next highest 10 after 57 is 60"). Call out numbers quickly but don't say the student's name until you have given the number. For example, "42 .... Billy." Response: "The partner to 10 is 8 so the answer is 50."

- Using the dice again have the groups of two children shake both dice, multiply the two numbers, and then give the next highest 10. For example, the numbers 6 and 3 are on the dice. Multiplied they are 18 and the next highest 10 is 20 because 2 is 8's partner to 10.

- "Count-by's" are a great way to build verbal competency. You will need to mediate this activity. Remember, our goal is clear oral language. Instruct the class to count by 7's beginning with 19. You will train them to watch your eyes to see who will be next. The first student you nod your head to will say 19. The next will say 26. Then you ask, "How did you get from 19 to 26?" Expect the response to go something like this: "I know that 1 is 9's partner to 10 so I went 1 more to 20. Then there were six left so I landed on 26." Look at the next student and the reply should be 33. Ask the student to defend his answer by explaining the process. "I know 4 is 6's partner to 10 so I went up to 30 and then 3 more because 4 and 3 are 7." Students are often able to do count-by's mentally, but explaining the process can be difficult. Work on it. You are building both verbal and cognitive fluency.

- Once students are adept at forward count-by's, have them go backward. For example, have them count backward from 94 by 11's. Talk first about their strategy. An easy one is to go back 10, then one more. This activity builds competence and confidence as well as inner language. And it's fun!

Propensity and potential.... Are you seeing the difference? As you build confidence in reluctant learners a new competence emerges, and that is worth infinitely more than a sticker on the page. Success in doing something difficult brings its own reward. We have not adjusted the curriculum downward for these students. We are expecting them all to perform. Our expectations are just above their level of functioning. Some will need more mediation than others, but that is our joy and pleasure. As master teachers we are becoming both artists and scientists.

REFLECTION

Because nothing was written down, the previous math activities relied on good auditory processing. This is usually a very weak area in our overstimulating visual culture. But thanks to what we know about cognitive modifiability, we can strengthen weak auditory systems. As we close this chapter, here is how we can do it with an Aesop fable.

The Fox and the Snake

 In crossing a river, a snake was carried away by the current. He managed to wriggle into a bundle of thorns that was floating by. A fox caught sight of it from the bank as it went whirling along. He cried out, "Oh my, the passenger fits the ship!"

There are just four sentences in this fable. In addition to its richness in moral lessons, it lends itself to the stimulation and strengthening of auditory processing.

- Ask the class to listen carefully while you read them a short paragraph, one sentence at a time. You may mention that it is a fable. Read the first sentence clearly and with expression. Simply say, "Now repeat." Have the students repeat it in unison. Now ask if one or two students would like to try that sentence alone. Then you repeat it again, and then have them say the sentence in turns to a partner. There should be no visual input at this time.

- Now read the second sentence followed by the words, "Repeat." You may want to repeat it if responses are weak. Remember, auditory memory is not strong in most students so aim just above their functioning but not so high as to frustrate. This may be all you try the first time.

- Once they have repeated the second sentence orally to a partner, have them orally put the two sentences together. Then see if they can write the sentences on their papers individually. After writing, have them compare with their partner.

- Put a transparency of the fable up for them to proof their work, checking for spelling, word order, and punctuation.

- If your class seems to be capable of repeating and writing the whole paragraph, take them there. This is hard to do but it becomes a great confidence builder.

Recognizing propensity is very freeing. Are you beginning to believe that this school year can be different from any other? Let's rediscover the reason we became teachers in the first place. Let's rediscover the joy!

CHAPTER TEN

REDISCOVERING THE JOY

"We serve the children because they are our spiritual betters. We teach them because they are our teachers."

R. C. SPROULE

URING THE six years I spent teaching children in Stoke Poges infant and middle schools in England I discovered a skylight. These young struggling learners taught me much more than I could ever have taught them. From them I began to understand some of the complexities of the struggle between intellectual competence and weak and vulnerable cognitive systems. Once these systems were strengthened, once they learned how to learn, the casualties in confidence and competence improved dramatically. All this was before I had ever heard the term *learning disabilities*. I was in my own quiet schoolroom in a tiny English village with no worksheets or workbooks to fall back on. Through the struggles, the skylight gradually opened.

I began to realize the solutions when I recognized that these students were always surprising me with their competence, cleverness, and unique giftedness. When I stopped adjusting my expectations downward and raised them just a bit, they consistently rose to the next level. I learned that teachers can inspire hope simply by saying, "This is hard but I know you can do it. Let's get there together."

Without knowing the terms *cognitive modifiability, zone of proximal development,* or *mediated learning*, my unique laboratory of nineteen struggling learners ushered me into these principles. You might say I rediscovered the true joy of teaching. I am deeply indebted to the children of Stoke Poges, wherever they are today.

Our family returned to the United States on our last set of military orders, but I had another in my pocket. It had turned into a huge gold coin. For I had developed a strong belief in the power of educational change and I was prepared to spend the rest of my life teaching students how to learn, not just what.

Have you had such a defining moment in your life? A moment when you knew this job of teaching was what you were destined for? When you understood that the struggles were meant to reshape you and give you a special kind of iron in your soul? When you began to delight in the uniqueness of all learners, not wish they all looked like the high performers?

In this chapter we are going to glance back at the concepts presented in the first nine chapters. It's kind of a review for the final test!

WHAT IS YOUR SKYLIGHT?

As you read this book, did you realize that your cognitive abilities are in the process of dynamic change? Have you recognized your own intellectual skylights? They have something to do with your innate gifts, the way you think and reason. This illumination may have come in a flash of insight, an "aha" moment. Skylights represent your ability to transcend all that you have been taught about teaching and learning and to step bravely into new territory, where you have never been before. They shine light into the dark corners of outdated ideas and stuffy routines. They put worksheets in their place. They represent an upward glance, fresh hope in the struggle.

Your skylight may begin with a new understanding that your best teaching days are ahead of you. The way forward becomes an illuminated path, with many cheering on the sidelines. For you often find your skylight in the company of others, discussing ideas. Often it will be your students who lead you there. Ultimately, you will recognize your skylight because you will sense in yourself a new freedom.

Have you begun to think of ways to ease the pressure of endless assessments and to relax more in your ability to help students learn and think by connecting to their own life experiences? When you begin to recognize your own confidence and competence in this area you place yourself on an ever-rising trajectory.

Remember, this transition to change the way you teach is a process, not an event. Much of your success in easing pressure has to do with your level of confidence on any given day. Once you know that all learners benefit from hearing their peers discuss thoughts, ideas, and strategies, you will have the incentive and confidence to initiate those unpredictable, open-ended discussions. The joy happens in the discovery, not in the planning of the oral discourse. Each day becomes a new adventure for teachers and students alike. The joy of really teaching students, not just presenting content, returns. And so will the smiles.

WHERE ARE THE SCHOLARS?

It goes without saying that there is a need for scholarship in the teaching profession. Teachers should be scholars. Let's define the term. A scholar is an individual who has a fund of knowledge or learning. What does this fund look like? It certainly involves the process of earning a degree, so there is an inner discipline built from years of taking courses, writing papers, and discussing academic subjects.

But it also implies compiling information about the field of education. People have been teaching and learning for centuries, but only relatively recently have we begun to understand the brain's role in the process. Keeping current in the latest advances in neuropsychology as well as the field of learning disorders is an important part of a teacher's scholarship.

The discipline of learning in an academic setting provides teachers with fundamental knowledge that has the power to connect learning to life. The specific discipline of writing papers is a sure way to improve language skills; writing involves much of the brain's circuitry. Even if you are not required to write papers for a course, consider jotting down your experiences in a journal. It will keep you witty and wise. If you are fortunate enough to be in a group of peers where oral language is valued and intellectual debate is encouraged, you are continually sharpening and refining language and questioning skills. A master's degree should be a gold coin in every teacher's pocket.

THE POWER OF THE FABLE

I have used the fables of Aesop throughout this book. Have you personalized them? A good exercise is to read them again and make personal applications to your life. This is higher-level thinking at its best, taking you into synthesis and evaluation, and stretching your cognitive abilities. Then you will be better able to lead students to draw lessons from their past that apply to their future. Find joy in the connections.

Are you taking time to read some of the great classic books for pleasure? There is something about the richness of language in these volumes that builds cognitive fluency. Plan to discuss the books you are reading with a friend. Discuss the themes, analyze the action, and exchange points of view. Such discussions improve oral competency and will make you a better teacher. If the only books you read are romance novels, you will need a bit more cognitive stimulation! Join a book club for fun and to stretch you beyond the academic demands of your second- or eleventh-grade class. You may even want to share the wisdom of a fable with friends.

CULTURAL RELEVANCY

Are you digging into the cultural relevancy of issues and bringing real-life situations into your lessons? As I write this book it is an election year in the United States. The issues that the candidates debate are rich fodder for the class-room. Current events should find their way into classroom discussions at least once a day. As should geography. Don't forget to work on those map skills. Use the graded dictionaries of cultural literacy (Hirsch, 1988) to reinforce awareness of the culture of your area, country, and world. Open those skylights.

How about modeling a love of learning for its own sake? Have you discovered ways to do that in your classroom? I like to share the story of my first experiences with Sudoku. This number game was invented in the United States in the 1970s but it really caught on in Japan in the 1980s, then spread around the globe. It is everywhere today. On a recent long journey I decided to try it but could not seem to get the hang of it. Then a friend bought me a beginner's book (this is actually a good place to start) and gently walked me through some strategies that helped me tremendously. Now I am hooked, and I really do think I am growing new dendrites! Try it. But get someone who is good to help you and do not start with the hardest ones or you will become discouraged. It has much to do with mediation—that is, direction from another adult.

Always be ready to try something new. You will be a much better teacher if you, yourself, are always learning.

STRUGGLING LEARNERS

What about those struggling learners? Do you feel better prepared to teach them? Are you raising the bar in your expectations for their success? As I have made clear, this is my special passion. Those who learn easily are going to get there without us, but helping a learner overcome barriers brings a special kind of joy. Work in collaboration with the specialists in your school. Helping struggling learners is a team event.

CONSIDER YOUR CLIMATE

What about your room arrangement? For some, placing students in pods may present difficulties, particularly if you have a noisy class. Many teachers are used to rows and are more comfortable with quiet learners, so the new ideas of student interactive dialogue may present a problem. You may find it easier to arrange students in pairs first, side by side, or perhaps ease into student interaction with a few of the more mature ones pairing up until you build a climate of discussion. Even if desks are not together, your room arrangement should enable students to connect meaningfully on a regular basis and discuss what they are thinking and learning. Students can find a place on the floor or a comfortable corner in which to work together. Regardless of your choice of room arrangement, make it a rule not to have students sitting at their desks continually doing independent work. Even the best minds can only absorb what the seat can endure. Get them moving, talking meaningfully, enjoying learning.

What about the atmosphere in your room? What do students see when they walk in? Clutter on walls and on your desk can be very distracting and for many it is visual overload. A few well-placed posters and attractive bulletin boards provide just the right amount of visual stimulation for most learners. Less is best. I suggest putting a model of the three-story intellect with skylight on display somewhere on one of your walls. This will remind students of their progress in building their intellectual skills. It is also a great idea to have a full-color poster of the human brain with labels visible to refer to regularly. "Building Better Brains" is a great motto that keeps learning in perspective beyond the inevitable test-taking.

WATCH YOUR LANGUAGE!

Are you becoming more comfortable with the process of using precise oral language to direct your students' thinking? Are your questioning skills improving? You may also want to post visuals of Bloom's taxonomy so that questions asked and answered can be analyzed quickly. A simple fact or reasoning visual is sufficient for the lower grades.

Is your class moving beyond memorization into dynamic discovery of ideas? Do they understand the difference between memorizing facts and discussing or reasoning to find answers? Do students recognize the importance of inner language to direct their thinking and actions? Another visual could relate to inner language with a simple question: "Inner language . . . have you used yours today?"

Have you discussed with students the difference between potential and propensity? You can illustrate these concepts with a box and a lid representing potential and a trajectory scaling ever upward to indicate unlimited possibility. These are terms students should be familiar with and feel comfortable discussing. Do they understand they have skylights? As you become more proficient in recognizing the skylight moments for your students, call them out. They will soon see them for themselves. Restoring the joy can become a daily experience.

As you assess these questions and your answers to them, there are some other issues that must be addressed if we are to rediscover the joy of teaching. Let's move into some very practical solutions to our fast-paced lifestyles.

FINDING MARGIN

I read a book some time ago called *Margin* by Richard Swenson (2004), a medical doctor. Swenson defines margin as the space between our load and our limits. It is that which is held in reserve for unanticipated situations. It is the gap between rest and exhaustion. It is the opposite of overload.

I suspect that if we were honest with each other we would admit there is very little margin in our busy lives. Teaching has a way of draining resources and failing to replenish them. I would like to make the case that margin is not just an unaffordable luxury. It is a necessity. So how do we find it?

It is fairly clear that margin is not going to be handed to us on a silver platter. We in the western world work harder and longer hours than any generation in history. You might say we are driven by those who worked hardest to get to the top and are now making the rules for the rest of us. If I want margin in my life, then I must create it. Here are some ideas that I have developed with the help of Swenson that apply specifically to teachers.

- Make it a general rule not to bring work home in the evenings. Stay at school as long as you need to for next-day planning. Keep your evenings for family or personal fun times.

- Plan mini holidays with your spouse or a good friend two or three times during the school year. These could be overnight getaways or a weekend in a restful place. They become gold coins in your pocket that you can plan for and anticipate during long stretches of hard work.

- Plan at least one two-week vacation each summer. Nothing refreshes like an extended time away from the routine. These do not have to be expensive adventures. The secret is to make them longer than a week. Every five years do a two-week getaway without the children as you celebrate special wedding anniversaries. The memories of these times are woven into your mind and heart providing lots of margin as you reflect on them in the busier days.

- Protect your weekends. Learn to say no to margin stealers. Be especially wary of committees and long-term commitments. Saying no is not selfish, rude, or insensitive. It is a preferred way of adhering closely to your priorities. Protect your time.

- Technology is responsible for stealing margin. Go on strike occasionally. Find the off switch.

- Recognize if you are in overdrive. In cars, this gear is only for when you need quick speed to pass someone. Yet many of us stay in this gear much too long. Move toward balance in physical rest. Ease up on the throttle. Plan some downtime.

- Let physical activity and sufficient sleep be margin restorers. Take action if you are not recognizing these friends.

- Learn to be content with what you have. It is amazing how this mindset can relax you and provide much needed margin from frantic shopping trips.

- Purpose to restore broken relationships. These steal margin regularly because of the emotional weight they cause.

- Learn to smile often and try to say "I'm wrong" or "I'm sorry" at least twice a day.

The ability to restore reserves to your overloaded life is yours. No one else can do it for you. As you begin to act on some of these suggestions you will rediscover joy in surprising places. Your family will be the primary beneficiaries, but your students will benefit also.

ONE MORE FABLE

The Goose That Laid the Golden Eggs

 A man and his wife had the good fortune to possess a goose that laid a golden egg every day. Lucky though they were, they soon began to think they were not getting rich fast enough. Imagining the bird must be made of gold inside, they decided to kill it in order to secure the whole store of precious metal at once. But when they cut it open they found it was just like any other goose. Thus, they neither got rich all at once, as they had hoped, nor enjoyed any longer the daily addition to their wealth.

This is a sad story that relates to both greed and margin. So often we want more than we have even though our containers are quite full. Students today seem to have a collective ambition to become either rich or famous. Both have the potential to be margin stealers.

It would seem that lessons in contentment are very important for young people today. We need to be role models for this exceptional trait. This fable might be a good place to start. You could do a contentment survey through a discussion on the lesson Aesop was teaching. Creating margin is not just for adults. Many of our students need to find and develop it as well. The creation of margin restores joy almost immediately. Try it. Plan a vacation or come off that committee.

PROFESSIONAL JOY RESTORERS

Begin to summarize your professional strengths. Be generous with yourself. Make a list of qualities you have either because of natural endowment or professional training. Try to extend your list to five to seven strengths. Then, quietly, in a moment of delicious margin, celebrate each one because your strengths have benefited many students. Take your list to a trusted colleague who has also created a list and share each of your professional strengths. See if you can add a few to your colleague's list that he did not name. Affirm one another. If there is great trust established between the two of you, you can also discuss weaknesses. But save that for another day.

Throughout this book we have discussed recognition of gifts within teachers who are coworkers. Some are particularly strong in certain areas. Talk to a principal about sharing the wealth, observing talent, learning from one another. All students benefit from such collaborative efforts. New teachers, particularly, should be assigned a strong mentor. Joy is contagious. So is misery. Be careful which you perpetuate. Purpose to choose joy.

Ongoing coursework is important to keep teachers' minds sharp and keep us current in new knowledge emerging in our field. I believe all teachers should pursue graduate degrees that affirm our high calling and professionalism. Be careful not to let this pursuit interfere with margin you are creating, however. Go slowly, wisely. Online options are wonderful today.

I have mentioned the difficulty that some adults, even successful teachers, have in reading for pleasure. This problem can be corrected with some focused work. Can you imagine the joy of being set free from a reading or learning problem after many years of frustration? And think how it will enrich your teaching. Pursue this avenue. You will be glad you did. Reading specialists are the best choice here, not tutors.

Suppose oral language is not your strength. This, too, can be developed. One of the best ways to improve oral language is to take a public speaking course. You will be given practice under a knowledgeable coach to become more proficient in this important skill. The companion skills of reading and writing have been shown to also help develop oral speech despite the fear that Socrates had. The more you read and write the more fluent you become in oral language. Become involved in small groups that allow and encourage dialogue. Ask a colleague to let you talk through a particular issue and help mediate your oral language.

For some, the problem is not limited oral speech; rather, it is unfocused, random speech. This too can be mediated by a trusted friend or colleague. Using the principles we have covered together in this book, open yourself to developing more focused, clear speech by practicing your dialogue. Often, it is very helpful to use a video- or audiotape to help listen to yourself. Difficult, but helpful. If we are sincere about becoming better teachers we will use any tool at our disposal. Cognitive modifiability is a great gift.

MY CLOSING CHAPTER

I have just returned from a most amazing adventure in South Africa. My husband and I took one of those two-week vacations (anniversary forty-five) that I will treasure for as long as I live. We went to a private game reserve, where we saw lions, rhinos, elephants, giraffes, hippos, wildebeests, warthogs, impala, and a host of other creatures. We had the awesome experience of watching lion cubs feeding on a recent kill and having our open vehicle surrounded by the deadliest animal in Africa, the Cape buffalo. We stood under the stars in the southern sky and saw the Milky Way, and the Southern Cross, which is invisible to us in the Northern Hemisphere. And we walked to the end of the earth at the Cape of Good Hope where the Atlantic and Indian Oceans meet.

At the end of our two weeks I presented at a conference of medical and educational professionals who had joined together to learn more about how best to reach and teach children. It does not get any better than this! All this because of the joy of discovery.

Teachers must learn to anticipate real life adventures. Make a list of the things you would love to do one day. Just making the list is a joy restorer. Then, wait for the surprises.

A FINAL WORD

My husband, two daughters, and I came back to Norfolk, Virginia, in 1983, wondering what we would do with ourselves after a twenty-year career in the navy. We had certainly seen the world, as promised by the navy motto, and our taste for adventure remained strong. Yet we had no idea of the amazing doors that were ready to open and the remarkable discoveries that awaited us. In fact, over the next twenty years we were each drawn into the field of education along quite different paths.

After retiring from the navy my husband became a much loved elementary school administrator. Our oldest daughter earned her master's degree in special education and has been teaching children with special needs for several years. I have learned a lot from her experience. Our youngest daughter received her master's degree in speech and language pathology and is now a trainer of teachers in how-to-learn methods. Our adventures in Thailand and England broadened our horizons and gave us the passion to bend and to serve students who are indeed our spiritual betters. This adventure keeps getting more and more joyful.

My adventure culminated with my training in Virginia in 1984 to become an educational therapist, a most gratifying career. Like the professions of clinical specialists such as physical therapists, occupational therapists, and speech and language therapists, this field of educational therapy provides tools of intervention that produce skylights for struggling learners and their teachers. It brings the satisfaction of knowing that root problems in learning can be addressed beyond just treating symptoms. The unusual synergy of our family interactions increases our corporate joy in this wonderful work of restoration.

Journeys are important. You may not need to go very far to benefit from an adventure. But you must keep moving forward. From England, to Bridgeville, to Virginia, to California, to Bangkok, to England, and back to Virginia again, my own journeys have destined me to make a difference in the lives of children. I believe yours will too. For as you incorporate some of the lessons from this book you open yourself to adventures undreamed of. Take a risk. Step out of the ordinary. Become the teacher you have always dreamed of being. Your skylight beckons.

REFERENCES

American Psychological Association. *Intelligence: Knowns and Unknowns* (Task Force Report). Washington, D.C.: American Psychological Association, 1995.

Ashliman, D. *Aesop's Fables*. New York: Barnes & Noble Classics, 2003.

Barkley, R. *ADHD and the Nature of Self-Control*. New York: Guilford Press, 1997.

Brooks, R., and Goldstein, S. *Raising Resilient Children*. Chicago: Contemporary Books, 2003.

Caine, R., and Caine, G. *Making Connections: Teaching and the Human Brain*. Alexandria, Va.: ASCD, 1991.

Campioni, J. "Assisted Assessment: A Taxonomy of Approaches and an Outline of Strengths and Weaknesses." *Journal of Learning Disabilities,* 1989, *22*, 151–165.

Cattell, R. B. *Intelligence: Its Structure, Growth and Action*. New York: Elsevier, 1987.

Evans, J. *An Uncommon Gift*. Philadelphia: Bridgebooks/Westminster Press, 1983.

Feuerstein, R. *The Dynamic Assessment of Cognitive Modifiability*. Jerusalem: International Center for the Enhancement of Learning Potential (ICELP), 2002.

Feuerstein, R. *The Feuerstein Instrumental Enrichment Program*. Jerusalem: ICELP, 2006.

Feuerstein, R. "Elaboration of Mediated Learning Experience." Paper presented at the ICELP, Paris, July 2007.

Feuerstein, R., and Falik, L. "Thinking to Learn; Learning to Think." forthcoming.

Feuerstein, Rafi. "The Coherence of the Theory of Modifiability." In R. Feuerstein, R. Feuerstein, and A. Kozulin (eds.), *The Ontogeny of Cognitive Modifiability*. Jerusalem: ICELP, 1997.

Gardner, H. *Multiple Intelligences: The Theory in Practice*. New York: Basic Books, 1993.

Healy, J. *Endangered Minds*. New York: Touchstone, 1990.

Healy, J. *Failure to Connect*. New York: Touchstone, 1999.

Hirsch, E. D. *Dictionary of Cultural Literacy*. Boston: Houghton Mifflin, 1988.

"History Place." http://www.historyplace.com/worldhistory/famine/introduction.htm. 2008.

Holmes, O. W. *The Poet at the Breakfast Table*. Boston: Houghton Mifflin, 1993. [originally published 1882]

Luria, A. R. *The Working Brain*. New York: Basic Books, 1973.

Mastopieri, M. "Keynote Address." Presentation at the Learning Disabilities Association conference, Chicago, 2008.

McCain, J. *Character Is Destiny: Inspiring Stories Every Young Person Should Know and Every Adult Should Remember*. New York: Random House, 2006.

Meredith, R. *The Elephant and the Dragon: The Rise of India and China and What It Means for All of Us*. New York: Norton, 2007.

Minirth, F. *A Brilliant Mind: Proven Ways to Increase Your Brainpower*. Grand Rapids, Mich.: Revell, 2007.

Moats, L. "Preparing and Supporting Teachers of Reading." Paper presented at the International Dyslexia Association (IDA) conference, Chicago, 2006.

Mutzabaugh, G. *A Work of His Grace: The Development of the National Institute for Learning Disabilities*. Norfolk, Va.: National Institute for Learning Disabilities, 1999.

Narrol, G., and Giblon, S. *The Fourth R: Uncovering Hidden Learning Potential*. Baltimore: University Park Press, 2001.

Norris, S. *The Generalizability of Critical Thinking*. New York: Teachers College Press, 1992.

Piaget, J. *The Language and Thought of the Child*. New York: Humanities Press, 1959.

Reeves, D. *Reframing Teacher Leadership* Alexandria, Va.: ASCD, 2008.

Silver, A., and Hagin, R. *Disorders of Learning in Childhood*. New York: Wiley, 2002.

Skinner, B. F. *The Behavior of Organisms*. New York: Appelton-Century-Crofts, 1938.

Swenson, R. *Margin*. Colorado Springs, Colo.: Navpress, 2004.

Tucker, M. "Charting a New Course for Schools." *Educational Leadership*, 2007, *64*(*7*), 48–52.

Vygotsky, L. *Thought and Language*. Cambridge, Mass.: MIT Press, 1994.

Welty, E. *One Writer's Beginnings*. Cambridge, Mass.: Harvard University Press, 1984.

Will, E. J. "Handwriting and Signatures: Some Basic Facts and Theory." http://www.qdewill.com/theory.htm. 2005.

Wolf, M. "Proust and the Squid." In *The Story and Science of the Reading Brain*. New York: HarperCollins, 2007.

Wooden, J., and Carty, J. *Pyramid of Success Playbook*. Regal Books: Ventura, Calif., 2005.

INDEX

A

Achievement, students' ridicule of, 69

Active working memory. *See* Working memory

Adventures, 149, 150

Alphabet, 103, 127

American Psychological Association, 5

Analysis: dominance of, 53–54; fable regarding, 62–64; versus synthesis, 53–57

Ashliman, D., 15

Atlantic Monthly magazine, 70

Attentional deficit, 117

Auditory processing, 136–137

Autistic students, 30

B

Barkley, R., 117

Base ten system, 135

Beauty, 3

Behavior problems, 99, 100, 117

Behaviorism: description of, 28; versus modifiability, 30

Beliefs: cognitive modifiability and, 31; as guide to practice, 4; parents' influence on, 15

Bloom's taxonomy, 53

Boredom, in classrooms, 75

Brain, human: deterioration of, 29–30; executive function of, 117–118; grammar and, 121; handwriting and, 61–62; importance of social interaction to, 30; influence of television and video games on, 59; memory systems in, 97–99; open architecture of, 57; scholarship in research of, 143; spatial maps and, 104; stimulating language areas in, 59–60; students' interest in, 72; surface versus meaningful knowledge and, 29

Brick building theory: description of, 5–6; teaching fables and, 15–19

Bridgeville Consolidated School, 55

Bridging, xiii

Brooks, R., 41

Bulletin boards, 145

Bury St. Edmonds school, 13–14

C

Caine, G., 25, 28, 101

Caine, R., 25, 28, 101

Campioni, J., 10–11

Carey, P., 40, 103

Carty, J., 37

Cast building theory: description of, 5; teaching fables and, 16–19

Categorizing: benefits of, 18; in fable lessons, 18; grammar and, 121

Cattell, R. B., 6

Change: confidence and, 47; intellectual potential and, 10–11, 15; learning through, 3–4; personal experiences and, 30; process of, 142; in theories of intelligence, 5–8

Character Is Destiny: Inspiring Stories Every Young Person Should Know and Every Adult Should Remember (McCain), 85

China, 25

Churchill, W., 85–90

Classic literature, 94, 143

Classroom environment: grouping students in, 57; joy of teaching and, 144–145; moveable walls in, 100

Cleverness, 5

Cluttered classrooms, 145

Cognitive capacity, 101

Cognitive competence: description of, 131–132; deterioration of, 128–129; mediating a feeling of, 131–136; memory building and, 99; teachers' reflection on, 41; teachers' self-assessment of, 47; teaching fables to develop, 17–19

Cognitive map, xii

Cognitive modifiability: versus behaviorism, 30; classroom applications regarding, 31–34; definition of, 11; importance of, 29–30; intellectual propensity and, 129; love of reading and, 43

Competence. *See* Cognitive competence

Competition, in classroom activities, 34, 91

Computers, for writing activities, 60

Conclusions, drawing, 54

CPSIA information can be obtained at www.ICGtesting.com
Printed in the USA
BVOW02n1457141214

378813BV00005B/8/P